IMAGES
of America

OHIO VALLEY
POTTERY TOWNS

FOR MY MOTHER AND DOROTHY

IMAGES
of America

OHIO VALLEY
POTTERY TOWNS

Pamela Lee Gray

ARCADIA
PUBLISHING

Published by Arcadia Publishing
Charleston, South Carolina

Library of Congress Catalog Card Number: 2002111096

For all general information contact Arcadia Publishing at:
Telephone 843-853-2070
Fax 843-853-0044
E-mail sales@arcadiapublishing.com
For customer service and orders:
Toll-Free 1-888-313-2665

Visit us on the Internet at www.arcadiapublishing.com

CONTENTS

Thompson Pottery Co., East Liverpool, Ohio.

A CACOPHONY OF KILNS, EAST LIVERPOOL, C. 1880. (Museum of Ceramics.)

INTRODUCTION

The natural resources of the Ohio River Valley provided a perfect location for the creation of the American crockery industry. The earliest potters arrived from England, Ireland, and Scotland, having been trained in their homelands before they emigrated. Letters home boasted that wares sold quickly and for top dollar, and this brought an abundance of skilled immigrant workers for the developing industry.

The lands of Pennsylvania yielded clays and a ready supply of salt for the single and two-person works around Beaver and Vanport. Entrepreneurial immigrants gained valuable experience at the local firms and were introduced to the latest innovations. Many left to establish their own works, often purchasing abandoned plants as bases for these new companies. As the new potteries expanded westward, the smaller works in Beaver County closed, unable

THE RICH CLAYS OF THE OHIO VALLEY. (Museum of Ceramics.)

to keep pace with the high volume of production and the large capacity of the East Liverpool factories. As production peaked, the land between the river and the hills was valued at a premium. Companies established branches or left for the nearby towns of Newell, Chester, and Wellsville.

A complete listing of potteries in the Ohio Valley would be impossible to record. Works were bought and sold numerous times, sometimes in a matter of months. Business partners merged and boards of directors overlapped. In many cases, pottery company records have disappeared or were destroyed by the frequent factory fires. Small one or two-person works were widespread, but these were rarely listed in city directories or official records.

The images in this book provide only a small glimpse of the pottery cities of Wellsville, East Palestine, and East Liverpool, Ohio; Beaver, Pennsylvania; and Newell and Chester, West Virginia. Photographs preserved by historical societies, libraries, museums, and family members tell a story of the people and towns. Periodicals, advertisements, and correspondence preserved from the period document the issues and crises that faced these villages. But the largest body of historical treasures exists in the surviving crockery. Decorative Lotus ware, with its fine, detailed design, is very different from early salt-glazed pottery meant for storage and everyday use. Utility ware was abundant, but it was damaged or destroyed through heavy use or later discarded as unworthy of preservation. Both types are highly collectible today and are widely displayed in museums.

Photographs open a precious historical window into the bustling valley. Trolleys and trains carried residents to work and to nearby towns for amusement and entertainment. Pottery workers made excellent wages and were purported to be the best-dressed residents in town. They could afford the services of stores, restaurants, and tailors, and these businesses grew as the ceramic industry expanded. Grand commercial structures and comfortable homes were built. All through the golden years, the expansive pottery works crowded the banks of the Ohio River, a reminder of the contribution that the industry made to the region's prosperity.

THE OHIO VALLEY: A REGION OF HILLS AND KILNS.

One

THE POTTER
AND THE TRADE

THE TRADE. The jolly, slip, board, stilt, bung, color, sagger, oven, or monkey were used by the thrower, chippers, fireman, dipper, turner, whirler, sitters-up, or decorators to create hollow ware, biscuit ware, and glost ware. These were the terms used to describe the tools, workers, and processes in the manufacture of crockery. While some of the words continue to be used in today's industry, other terminology was lost as machines took over tasks formerly done by hand. Machinery, while eliminating some jobs, allowed the industry to expand, creating an affordable, abundant product and a new working vocabulary. (Museum of Ceramics.)

THE POWER WHEEL. "Practical Potters" were skilled in many areas of the industry: Kiln building, model making, pressing, and glazing were all processes that required a minimum of three to five years of training before a title would be given to the worker. New hand-held tools and simple machines powered by foot, hand, or animals added another component to craft. By the 1860s, the works in the East Liverpool area were steam-powered. Between the production of the clay, forming and finishing the piece, firing, glazing, decal work, warehousing, and packing, numerous skilled and unskilled hands moved the ware along the process to a completed piece. (Allen County Public Library.)

THE WARE. Yellow ware and Rockingham were the first types of wares to be produced in the region. Made from local clays and fired with local coal, the pieces sold quickly to residents who previously had to rely on imported goods. Yellow and Rockingham ware fell out of fashion from 1870 until 1900 as American tastes turned to decals and patterns which could be featured on lighter ware. The industry moved to white ware and ironstone to meet fashions of the times. (Museum of Ceramics.)

THE POTTERY INDUSTRY. The potter was a craftsperson who trained and apprenticed to learn the art of creating pottery. In 1845, wage contracts were based on a complicated formula that included an average quota of 150 dozen of ware per week at payment of one dollar per score of 20 dozen. It averaged two to three dollars a week, which was considered a fair wage for the time. The potter was also required to give 30 days notice when leaving, or forfeit $20. Some contracts paid for work only every two to three months and early workers in the pioneer pottery industry took payment in ware or food and grain. (Cleveland Press Archive, Special Collections, Cleveland State University Library.)

PREPARING THE CLAY. One potter, his batter-out, runner, and his finisher working eleven days in 1904 hand-made 30,000 fruit dishes (2,550 dozen—an industry standard measurement) and 2,640 butter dishes (220 dozen). The average production was five fruits every minute with a butter thrown in almost every other minute. (Cleveland Press Archive, Special Collections, Cleveland State University Library.)

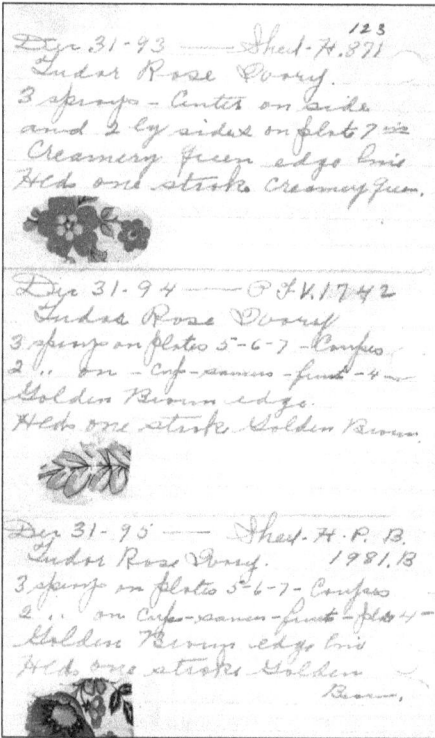

SECRET FORMULA FOR CLAY. The slip is the first mix of the clay. Liquid is added to the dry mixture and then poured through filters to screen out any impurities. Early potters kept intricate notebooks detailing "secret" clay formulas, decal selection, and test firing results. These small books identified the potter on the front cover and offered hefty rewards for the return of the notebook if it were to be lost or misplaced. (Museum of Ceramics.)

THE TURNER. Ernest Albert Sandeman in his text *Notes on the Manufacture of Earthenware* described the job of the turner in 1901: "Turning approaches more the work of an artist than to that of the workman, and the turner should have an accurate eye and a good idea of form, as for the most part the thrower or machine gives the thickness more or less, leaving it to a large extent to the turner to form and finish the piece." Sanderman maintained that expertly filed tools would produce the best turned ware. (Museum of Ceramics)

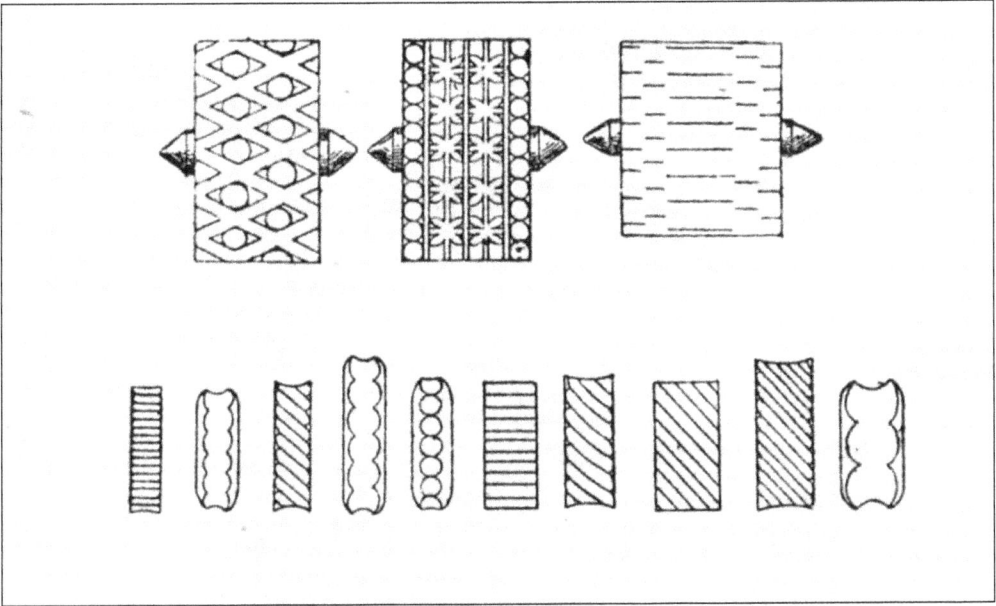

TOOLS: EMBOSSED ROLLERS AND THE WHEEL. The turner uses embossed rollers attached to the lathe to add patterns to the pottery piece. Turners would also add ornamentation such as lines, ribs, or grooves. The ideal piece should not be too moist or it might lose the shape. It should not be too dry or it might split when attached to the chuck (a round piece of wood where the piece is placed) on the lathe. Many lathes were driven by steam power by the turn of the century. (Gray Collection.)

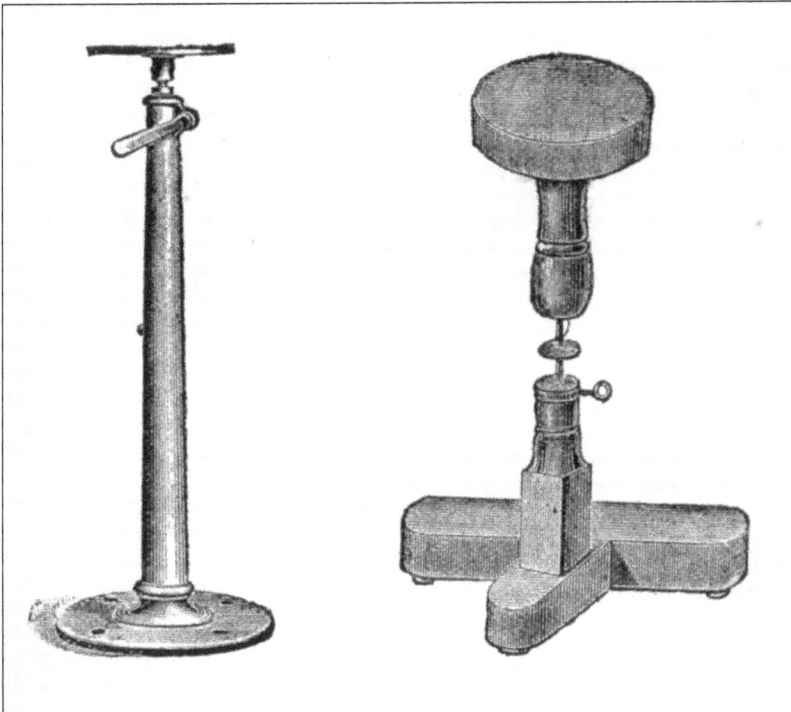

ASSEMBLY LINE MOLDING. Handmade pottery was "thrown" during the early years of manufacturing, but as demand increased and production was expanded, more molded pieces were produced. A liquid clay mixture was poured into forms or molds to cast the ware. (Cleveland Press Archive, Special Collections, Cleveland State University Library.)

TUMBLING THE WARE. Modern green ware is packed in a special silica sand before it enters a conveyor belt kiln for the bisque firing. After the first firing, the sand casting is removed by tumbling the ware through a heavy rubber inclined cylinder filled with abrasive pebbles. These clear the pieces to a smooth finish. (Courtesy of Sterling China.)

14

SANDBLASTING THE WARE. Delicate ware would be broken in the abrasive action of the kiln, so instead it is laid out on a wheel and pressure-sanded. The pieces then move on to be decorated. Prior to the introduction of machinery, all sanding processes were done by hand. (Courtesy of Sterling China.)

BISQUE WASHING MACHINE. The "underglaze print" is hand-engraved by an expert who then cuts the pattern into a copper cylinder. This is used to transfer color onto a continuous strip of thin tissue, which is cut and then placed onto bisque ware where it is brushed onto the piece. Finally the item is placed in water to wash away the tissue. (Forney Collection.)

HAND-LINED WARE, MAYER CHINA COMPANY, C. 1945. (Museum of Ceramics)

MACHINE LINER, C. 1960s. (Museum of Ceramics)

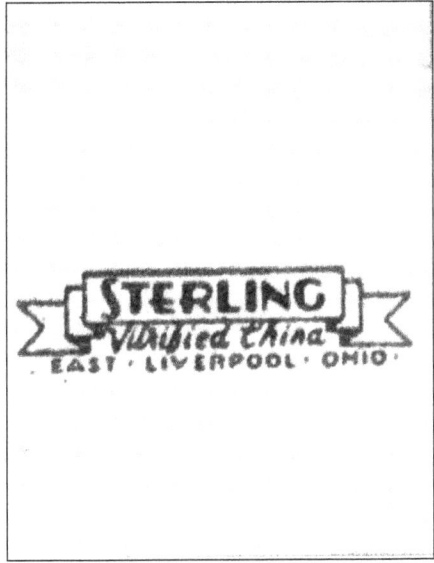

BACKSTAMPS. Pottery was frequently stamped with a maker's mark called a "backstamp." The term "vitrified" was applied to china that did not absorb moisture, a quality that was advantageous for restaurant and hotel ware. "Vitrified" was later used to denote commercial china meeting the sanitary requirements established by the federal government. It is primarily used on ware produced in America. (Gray Collection/Courtesy of Sterling China.)

DEVELOPING LINES AND PATTERNS. The goal of manufacturers is to create a line of ware that continues to retain popularity over the decades. Sterling's "El Rancho" is one such line. Manufactured for over 50 years, it continues in production today. (Courtesy Sterling China.)

AN EAST LIVERPOOL DECORATING SHOP, C. 1888. While potters were predominately male, the decorating shop employed mainly women. This photograph, donated to the Museum of Ceramics, sadly left workers unidentified. (Museum of Ceramics.)

REVOLVING STOVES, C. 1905. The ideal way to produce ware would be to fire each piece separately. Loss from imperfections in the clay during production, and from debris, would be minimal, but the cost would make the ware too expensive for resale—not to mention the impracticality of firing the kiln one piece at a time. To fire a number of pieces of ware, potters used thimbles, saddles, stilts, dumps, and ringer saggers to keep the wares from touching during the firing process. (Gray Collection/Museum of Ceramics.)

LOADING THE KILN AT THE HOMER LAUGHLIN CHINA COMPANY, C. 1906. Saggers were carried perfectly level so that ware would not fall off the various supports. A sagger loaded with plates weighs almost 75 pounds. Loaders had to avoid any bumps or jerking motions so that dust or sand would not fall into the saggers below. Either misstep would destroy the pieces as they were fired. This factory sales confirmation card illustrated the care HLCC took with their wares. (Museum of Ceramics.)

LOADING THE KILN. Modern firing is done in a fraction of the two to three days of the past. The kilns (pronounced "kill") no longer need to be cooled for the ware to be drawn. Saggers are loaded into the modern kilns operated at the Mayer works in Beaver Falls during the early 1950s. (Museum of Ceramics.)

THE SHIPPING SHED AT HARKER POTTERY, 1907. Workers take a break at the shipping shed. The structures where specialized decorating took place and from which china was shipped were separate from the main works. Samuel Orr, a crate repairman for John Goodwin, is given credit for the shift to barrels. He created a barrel in the pottery to substitute for the commonly-used crates. At only a fraction of the cost and with higher protection for the shipment, barrels soon became an industry standard. (Museum of Ceramics.)

Opposite: **THE LAST REMAINING BOTTLE KILN IN WELLSVILLE, 2002.** The fireman was responsible for testing the kiln for the best results and for keeping the fires burning evenly to produce quality wares. Large fresh lumps of coal were preferred to produce a long flame. The fireman was expected to keep watch through a "spy hole" in a beehive or milk bottle kiln to observe the color of the heat from the flues and the appearance of the interior of the oven. The trained and skilled fireman would observe varying degrees of change by the color of the brickwork and saggers. The duty of the sitters-in was to maintain an even heat while the fireman started and checked other kilns. Blistering occurred if the fire flashed. Uneven heat produced "feathering" of the glaze. Too much air drawn at any one time, an oven that "came up" to a high temperature very suddenly, failure to punch out the "clinkers" of coal, or "smoked ware" (blackened pieces resulting from a decrease in the amount of lead in the glaze), all meant unsaleable goods. Fear of disaster made some firemen "short-fire" their kilns. Short-fired ware produced a dull looking glaze that afterwards showed "crazing" or small cracks. A fireman's job was not easy. (Gray Collection.)

23

EAST LIVERPOOL POTTERIES ON THE SHORELINE OF THE OHIO RIVER. Pottery plants included separate structures for specialized use. Easy access to the river's edge was important for early firms that were loading ware onto barges and flatboats. Separate structures, where a horse walked in a circle pulling a beam to generate power, were used for stone grinding and clay mixing. (Museum of Ceramics.)

NAMING THE WORKS, THE PHOENIX POTTERY, C. 1949. Early pottery factories were called "works," with departments or "shops" named for their function, as in "clay" or "decorating." Many works had popular "works" names. The French China Company was called the "Klondike," a humorous reference to the length of the journey back to town after a day's work. Other plants were referred to by the name of their best-selling line of wares. "Phoenix," first opened as Woodward, Blakeley and Company, was an appropriate name for a factory in an industry where factory fires were common. A new works frequently rose from the ashes of another. (Museum of Ceramics.)

EMPLOYEES AT THE PHOENIX WORKS, C. 1900. (Museum of Ceramics.)

25

COAL TO FUEL THE POTTERY INDUSTRY. Prior to 1860, small amounts of coal were mined from hills in the area. This coal provided the fuel to fire the kilns of the early pottery industry. Carbon Hill, a New York-based firm, began operations with a railroad spur connected to the Fort Wayne Railroad line. This mine was abandoned in 1871, and Prospect Hill Coal Company and the State Line Coal Company opened large-scale operations. With the end of steam power for the railroads and the increased use of natural gas for industry, the demand for coal declined. Mines were abandoned as they ceased to be profitable. Natural gas and then electricity later powered potteries and other industries. (Gray Collection.)

THE HAZARDS OF NATURAL GAS FUEL. The Ohio Valley had excellent free resources of natural gas which were later used in place of coal to fire the kilns. Unfortunately, the volatility of the gas caused the destruction of many kilns, and sometimes spelled the end of an entire company. This photograph shows the damage at the Potters' Mining & Milling Company in East Liverpool in 1918. (Museum of Ceramics.)

IEW of SCIO POTTERY AFTER FIRE of 1947, SCIO, OHIO
Pub. by Gallagher's Pharmacy, Scio

AERIAL VIEW OF FIRE DAMAGE AT SCIO PLANT, OHIO, 1949. (Gray Collection.)

KEG PARTY AT ROCK SPRINGS C. 1900. The Harkers and their potters were ferried across the river to the park where they drank ten kegs of beer and danced to the music of the East Liverpool Brass Band. Happy pottery workers did not leave the firm. (Museum of Ceramics.)

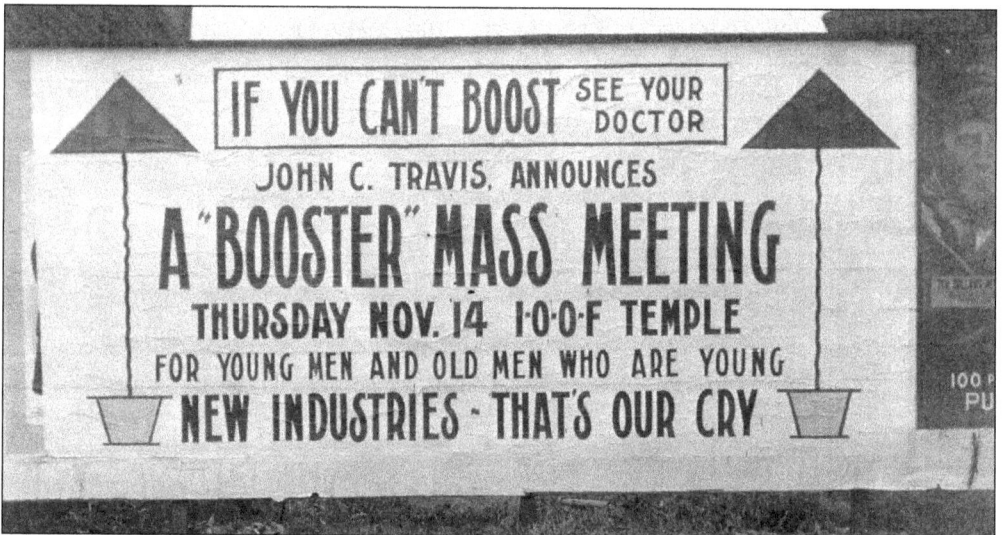

IF YOU CAN'T BOOST SEE YOUR DOCTOR

JOHN C. TRAVIS, ANNOUNCES

A "BOOSTER" MASS MEETING

THURSDAY NOV. 14 I·O·O·F TEMPLE

FOR YOUNG MEN AND OLD MEN WHO ARE YOUNG

NEW INDUSTRIES - THAT'S OUR CRY

PROMOTING AN INDUSTRY IN TOUGH ECONOMIC TIMES, C. 1918. The United States Potters' Association, formed in Philadelphia in 1875, had offices on Fourth and Market Streets in East Liverpool. The president was elected by the membership, and presidents of the larger companies of East Liverpool, East Palestine, Wellsville, Newell, and Chester were each elected to lead. The organization set prices and production limits for member works, in addition to promoting the pottery industry during times of economic decline. The collective maintained "The White Ware Compact" to maintain prices of goods, until it was broken in 1904. (Museum of Ceramics.)

BASKET PATTERN, C. 1920. Photographs of lines were carried by sales representatives and salesrooms at markets in Chicago, New York, and San Francisco. This decal pattern was produced at W.S. George in East Palestine. (Forney Collection.)

SALES BROCHURE, W.S. GEORGE, EAST PALESTINE, C. 1920S. Standard shapes were used for dinnerware. This brochure illustrates each of the basic shapes with the items offered in each line. Separate fliers displayed various decals, lining, and glazes that were available for this shape. Bolero was used by the George Company for many years. (Forney Collection.)

BOLERO

TRADE SHOWS. This industry publication shows W.S. George represented in New York and Chicago. Showrooms were important to sales. (Forney Collection.)

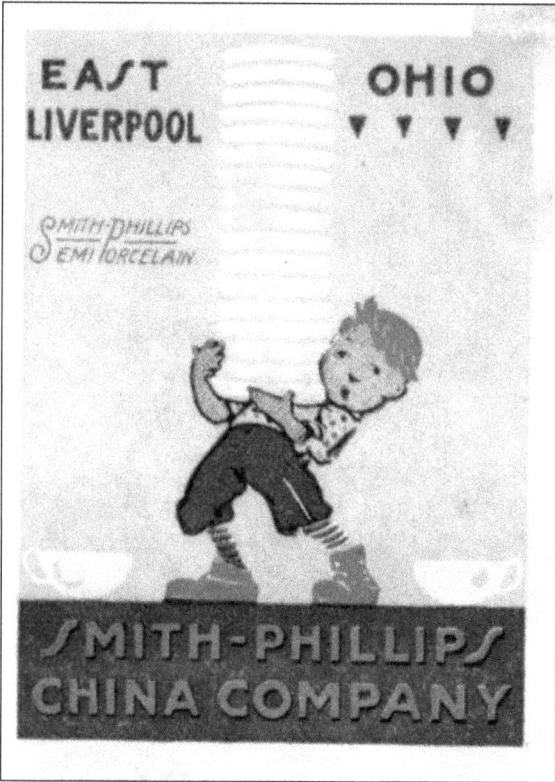

TRADE STAMPS. Smith & Phillips created a set of stylized stamps to attach to billings and factory mailings. (Museum of Ceramics.)

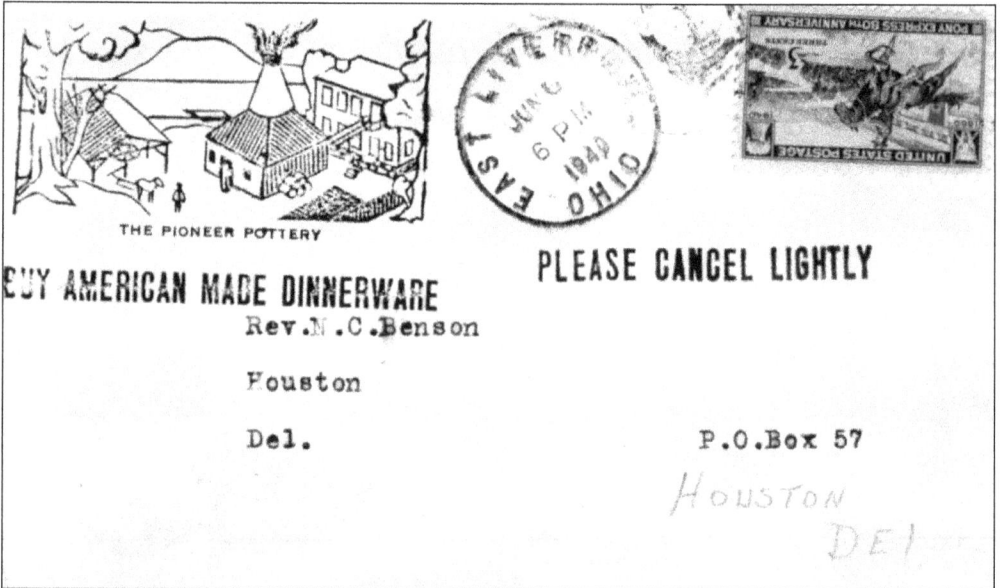

THE PIONEER POTTERY

BUY AMERICAN MADE DINNERWARE

Rev.M.C.Benson

Houston

Del.

PLEASE CANCEL LIGHTLY

P.O.Box 57

Houston
Del

UNITED STATES COMMEMORATIVE. A postal commemorative was issued in 1940. This first-day cancellation shows the beehive kiln of years past. (Gray Collection.)

TOURIST TRADE. Novelties, dishes, and dinnerware were popular items for purchase by visitors to the crockery cities. (Gray Collection.)

THE WEST COAST POTTERY TRADE. Ohio Valley pottery was sold in the West, in Canada, and overseas. (Gray Collection.)

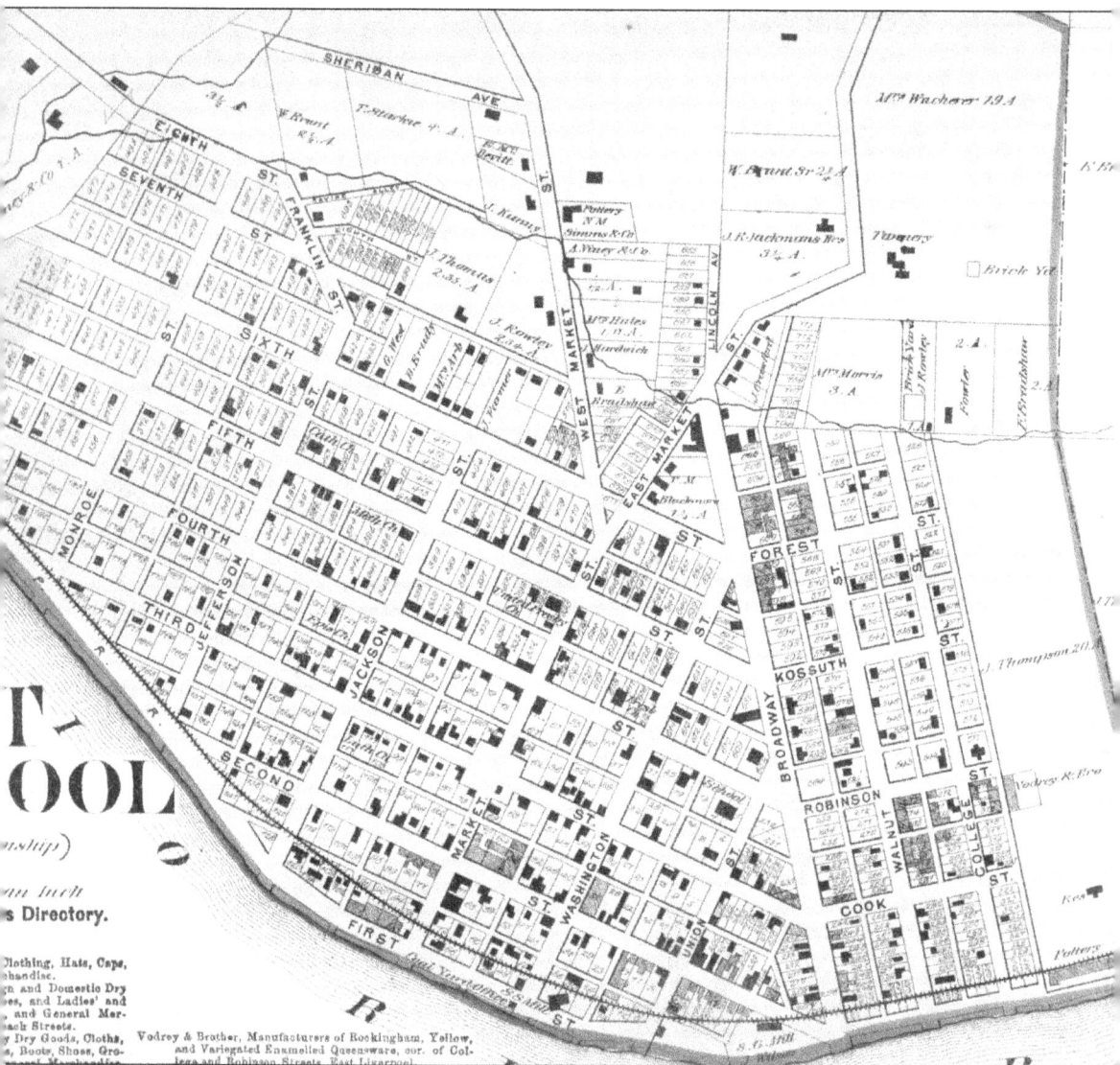

EAST LIVERPOOL, OHIO, C. 1870. (Allen County Public Library.)

Two

East Liverpool
Ohio

Welcome to the Crockery City. Isaac Craig purchased land at the point where Ohio, Pennsylvania, and West Virginia met under the terms of the Land Act of 1796. Thomas Fawcett bought over 1000 acres from Craig. Naming the area St. Clair, to honor the then-governor of the Northwest Territory, Thomas and Isabella Fawcett and their children settled in the area. The local residents insisted on calling the settlement "Fawcett's Town." This issue was later resolved when transplanted English potters incorporated the town as Liverpool in 1834. The state refused to recognize the new name, citing a Liverpool already existing in Medina County. The problem was solved with the addition of "East" a few years later. Soon after incorporation, the pottery industry developed to full production.

East Liverpool claims to have been the only community in the United States with an economic base of pottery and related products. Known as "The Crockery City," the town had over 200 potteries operating concurrently before the turn of the century.

The Pioneer Pottery
of East Liverpool, Ohio.

JAMES BENNETT AND REBECCA AT THE WELL TEAPOT. The first kiln was burned in 1840 by English immigrant James Bennett. He was joined by his brothers, Daniel, Edwin, and William, in producing Rockingham and yellow ware from a single kiln using the "Bennett's Liverpool Ware" mark. The company was located on the west end of Second Street. The firm relocated to Birmingham, Pennsylvania, in 1845. The first yellow ware mugs yielded a profit of $250, and with this first kiln of ware pottery as an industry in East Liverpool was born. (Museum of Ceramics.)

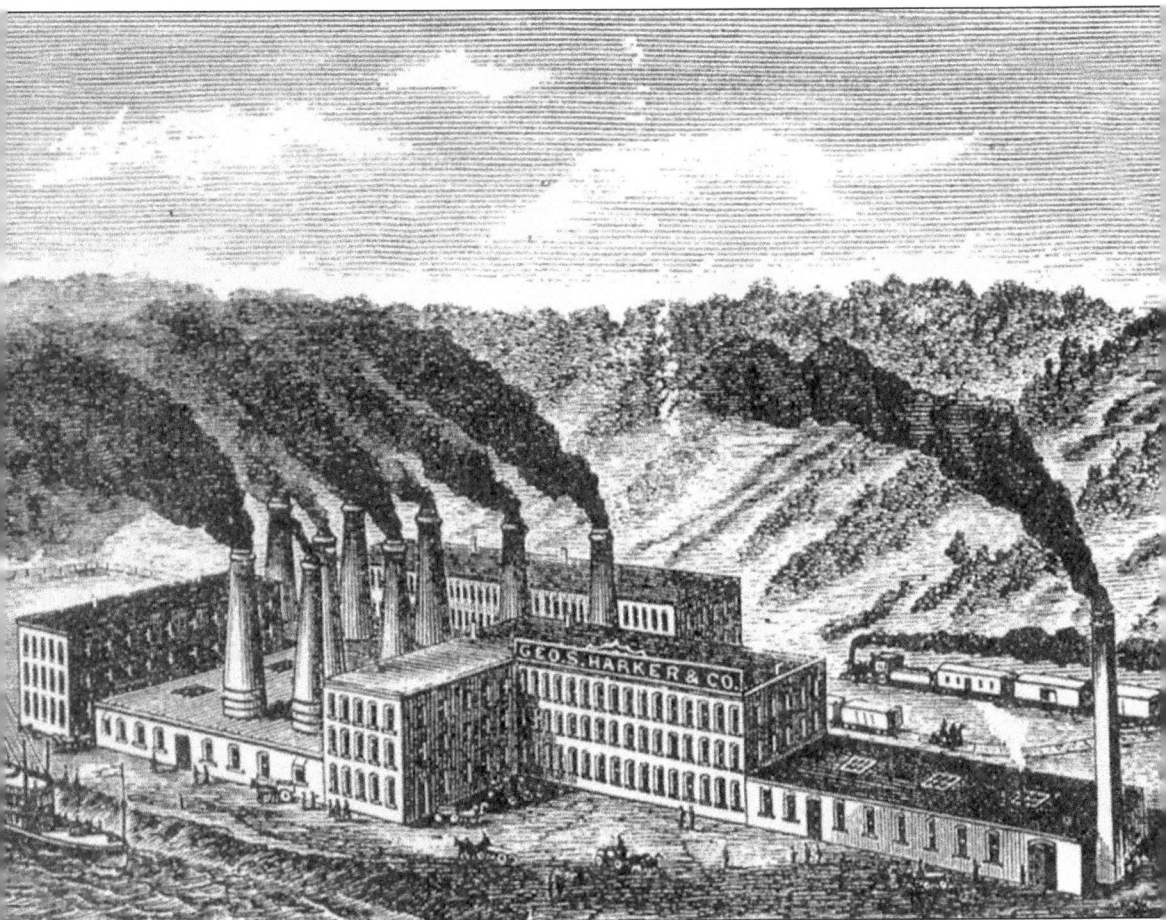

HARKER POTTERY COMPANY. Benjamin Harker Sr., grandfather to later presidents Benjamin Jr., William W., and H.W., established the second large-scale East Liverpool works in 1841. It was located on River Road. Edwin Tunnicliff, John Croxall, and John Goodwin leased the firm in 1842, but Harker took back the pottery less than a year later. With Goodwin's expertise and brother George S.'s fiscal contributions, the Etruria Works was partnered by James Taylor, David Boyce, and Thomas Fawcett over the years. Robert Harker and Charles R. Boyce, family members of the original owners, took control of the company in 1926. (Los Angeles County Library.)

HARKER POTTERY COMPANY. Benjamin Harker & Sons was established in 1840. This structure was built in 1877. The imprint on the mounting board states, "Wedgewood Pottery – Benjamin Harker and Sons, East Liverpool, Ohio." (Museum of Ceramics.)

THE BAGGOTT KNOB COMPANY. John Goodwin emigrated from England, and after living in other eastern cities, setled in East Liverpool. He worked at the Bennett Brothers and Harker plants before 1844, when he began producing Rockingham and yellow ware doorknobs at his own works located at Second Street and Pink Alley. Goodwin sold out to Samuel and William Baggott in 1853. The Baggots were recent immigrants from England. This factory was later taken over by Mountford and Son, makers of stilts and pottery supplies. (Los Angeles Public Library.)

BLOOR WARE AND WHITE WARE IN EAST LIVERPOOL. William Bloor is given credit for manufacturing the first white ware in 1860. Vases, mugs, and busts were all produced. Bloor cast most of the pieces made at their southeast corner plant at Walnut Street and High Alley. The factory closed in 1862 when male employees left to enlist for the Civil War. (Museum of Ceramics.)

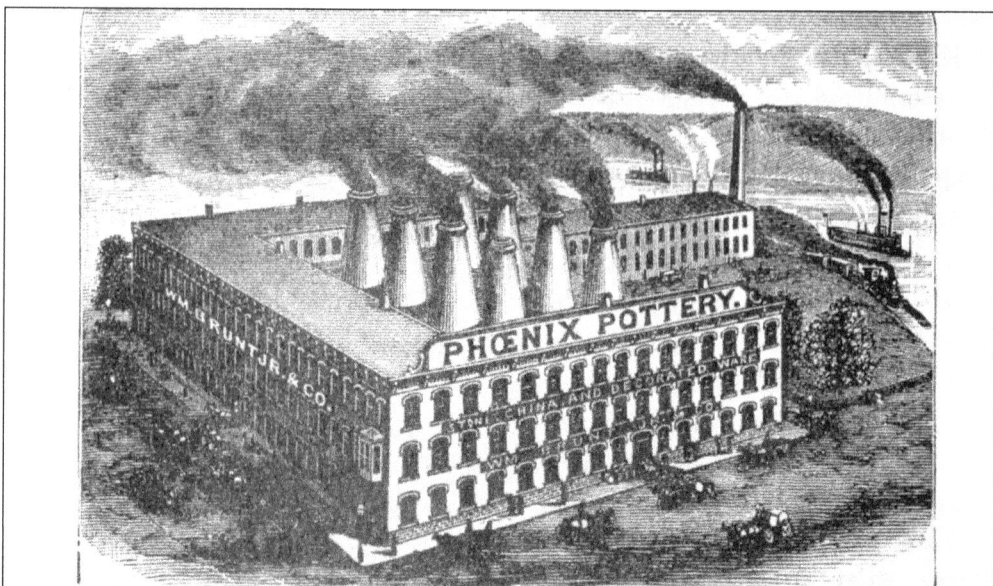

PHŒNIX POTTERY, WILLIAM BRUNT, JR., & CO., EAST LIVERPOOL, OHIO.

THE PHOENIX POTTERY. East Liverpool listed 11 potteries and 387 workers in 1853. Although many firms possessed only one kiln, Woodward, Blakeley and Company's "Phoenix Pottery" had three kilns with 40 employees. (Los Angeles Public Library.)

JOHN F. STEELE'S DECORATING ESTABLISHMENT.

JOHN F. STEELE'S DECORATING COMPANY, C. 1878. Many firms in town specialized in the application of decoration for wares. Steele's company, located on College Street, focused on chain, table, and toilet wares. (Los Angeles County Public Library.)

40

Firm Name.	Kind of Ware.	No. of Kilns.
Wm. Brunt, Jr., & Co	Stone-China.	5
Homer Laughlin	"	5
Knowles, Taylor & Knowles	"	5
Brunt, Bloor, Martin & Co	"	4
George S. Harker & Co	"	4
Godwin & Flentke	"	2
John Wyllie & Son	"	2
Vodrey Bros	"	2
Benj. Harker & Sons	C China.	2
West, Hardwick & Co	"	3
Goodwin Bros	"	3
C. C. Thompson & Co	Yellow-Ware.	5
Croxall & Cartwright*	"	4
Agner, Foutts & Co	"	4
S. & W. Baggott	"	3
Manley, Cartwright & Co	"	3
McNichol, Burton & Co	"	2
Flentke, Harrison & Co	"	1
Bulger & Worcester	"	2
McDevitt & Moore	"	2
Burford Bros	C China	1
H. Brunt & Son	Brown Door-Knobs.	2
Richard Thomas & Son	" " "	1

Total number of kilns............ 67

RIVERSIDE KNOB WORKS, C. 1945. Thirty to 40 workers turned out 80 barrels of knobs per week in this works in 1876. Each barrel held 1,500 to 1,800 knobs (depending on the knob design). Over three million knobs were produced each year. (Museum of Ceramics.)

H.S. Knowles. (signature)

KNOWLES, TAYLOR, AND KNOWLES. Isaac W. Knowles and Isaac A. Harvey began manufacturing Rockingham and yellow ware in 1853. Knowles bought out Harvey in 1867. John N. Taylor, Knowles' son-in-law, and his son H.S. joined the firm in 1872. With the addition of the new partners, the company began production of white granite ware. (Los Angeles Public Library.)

Isaac W. Knowles (signature)

THE LITTLE HOSTESS DINNER SET

COMPOSITION OF SET

Plates	6 Individual Butters
Cups	2 Covered Dishes
Saucers	1 Vegetable Dish
Fruits	1 Large Meat Dish
Creamer	1 Small Meat Dish
Sugar	

TAYLOR
SMITH &
TAYLOR CO

K.T.&K. The company bought the Bennett works located on Second Street and expanded to another factory on Walnut Street near East Sixth Street. They then enlarged the works again to Bradshaw Avenue and Walnut Street. With the introduction of the new partners, the firm became known as K.T.&K., which was incorporated into the company's backstamp. (Los Angeles Public Library.)

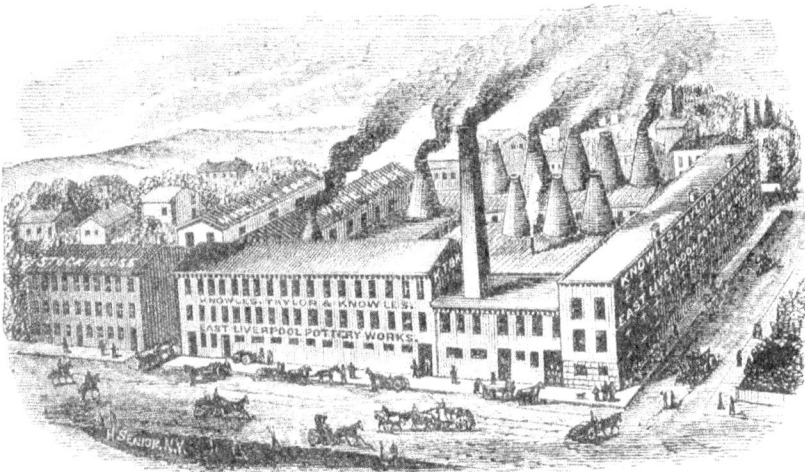

POTTERY WORKS OF KNOWLES, TAYLOR & KNOWLES, EAST LIVERPOOL, OHIO

HOMER LAUGHLIN CHINA COMPANY, EAST LIVERPOOL. Homer Laughlin China Company was founded in 1871 by brothers Homer and Stephen Laughlin on Little Beaver Creek, a few miles from East Liverpool. In 1872, they collected a bonus from the City of East Liverpool to establish a pottery to produce white ware to compete against imported crockery. Homer Laughlin China Company began in 1874 as the "Ohio Valley Pottery." Two years later the "Laughlin Brothers," Homer and Shakespeare, won top awards for their white ware at the Centennial Exposition in Philadelphia. This photo shows the new plant in Newell, West Virginia, billed as the "World's Largest." (Los Angles Public Library.)

THE
HALL CHINA CO.

Tea Pots and Cooking Ware

ZABETH and ANNA   **TEL. 385-2900**

THE HALL CHINA COMPANY. The East Liverpool Potteries Company was dissolved with Robert Hall accepting the plant on East Fourth Street and Walnut as his share of the company. West, Hardwick, and George Pottery had once operated from the same location. The Hall China Company was established there August 14, 1903. This city directory advertisement from the 1960s shows their present location on Anne Street. (Museum of Ceramics.)

ROBERT TAGGERT HALL. With his father's death only a year after starting the new company, Robert Taggert took over the firm in 1904. Hall was responsible for a unique lead-free, single fired glaze. The process took years to develop, but in 1910 the first successful mug was produced using a single firing. Company brochures, titled "Better Cooking," heralded Hall's unique nonporous, craze-proof "hollow ware." Hall developed a market during World War I that would ensure its survival during years of economic hardship. (Allen County Public Library.)

HALL CHINA, 1 ANNE STREET. Hall was one of the last pottery companies to move across the river to Chester and Newell, West Virginia. To the rear of the office is one of the last three remaining beehive kilns in the region. Company president John Sayle likens the kiln to "wearing a suspenders when you already are wearing a belt," simply a safety precaution. When the new plant was constructed in Newell, the new line kilns were the state-of-the-art in technology. Company owners wanted to insure uninterrupted supply and built the beehive as a backup kiln. It has never been used for ware. Today four roller-hearth German kilns provide state-of-the-art firing at the factory. (Gray Collection.)

ASSEMBLY LINE AT HALL CHINA. Ball jug pitchers roll off an assembly line in this photograph taken in 1937. (Cleveland Press Archive, Special Collections, Cleveland State University Library.)

HALL TEAPOTS, PITCHERS, AND HOLLOW WARE. Hall China Company, under the joint presidency of R.T. Hall and Francis Simmers, while continuing to make institutional and restaurant ware, began production of teapots in 1919. The firm soon became the world's largest retail marker of decorated teapots. Printed material provided with each teapot explained the importance of Halls' secret firing process and the best way to make tea. Robert T. Hall died in 1920 and Simmers took over the helm of the growing company which then saw a series of plant expansions, and in 1936, the addition of dinnerware. Two collector teapot designs were introduced in 2002. (Cleveland Press Archive, Special Collections, Cleveland State University Library.)

HALL PRODUCTION LINE. Hall routinely advertised in city directories promoting their special hollow ware. Today they hold 60 to 70 percent of the market in hollow ware manufacture. (Los Angeles County Library.)

C & P Railroad, c. 1907. Flooding halted all commerce at the tracks of the Cleveland and Pittsburgh Railroad on Second Street. Flooding was a constant problem in East Liverpool. The earliest pottery foundations located along the river have all been lost to the expanding Ohio River waters. (Museum of Ceramics.)

Riverview Greenhouses, "East Liverpool's Largest Florists," Anderson Blvd. Ph. 714, E. Liverpool, Ohio.

Alternative Uses for Abandoned Kilns, c. 1940s.

The Potters National Bank,
East Liverpool, Ohio.

POTTERS' NATIONAL BANK, C. 1900. The southwest corner of Broadway and Fourth Street was the location of the bank managed by William Brunt, president, John N. Taylor, vice president, and F.D. Kitchel, cashier. It was established in 1881 with board members: F.D. Kitchel, WIlliam and Joseph Cartwright, William Brunt, Jr., John N. Taylor, James H. Goodwin, and Noah Fredrick. (Museum of Ceramics.)

FIRST NATIONAL BANK. Banking and finance was an important facet of the pottery industry. The East Liverpool Banking Company was the first bank organized in the city. The institution began operating in 1872, but was charted a year later. The original office was located on the corner of Broadway and Second Streets where they paid Huff and Company $6,000 for the building and $125 for the furnishings. The Fifth Street building was constructed in 1922 at a cost of more than $260,000. (Allen County Public Library.)

Ties to
England.
Many potters
learned their
trade in
England and
ties remained
strong even
though they
had a new
home in the
Ohio Valley.
(Museum
of Ceramics.)

THE FLOOD OF 1918. Thompson's Pottery is shown during the major flooding of 1918. The postcard sender writes, "The river is back where it belongs now and everything is normal." Flooding was an ongoing problem for tri-state area towns. (Museum of Ceramics.)

CELEBRATION, C. 1918. L.S. Wilson Company, Milliners is featured prominently in this photo of a downtown Greek community parade. East Liverpool had a diverse population. (Museum of Ceramics.)

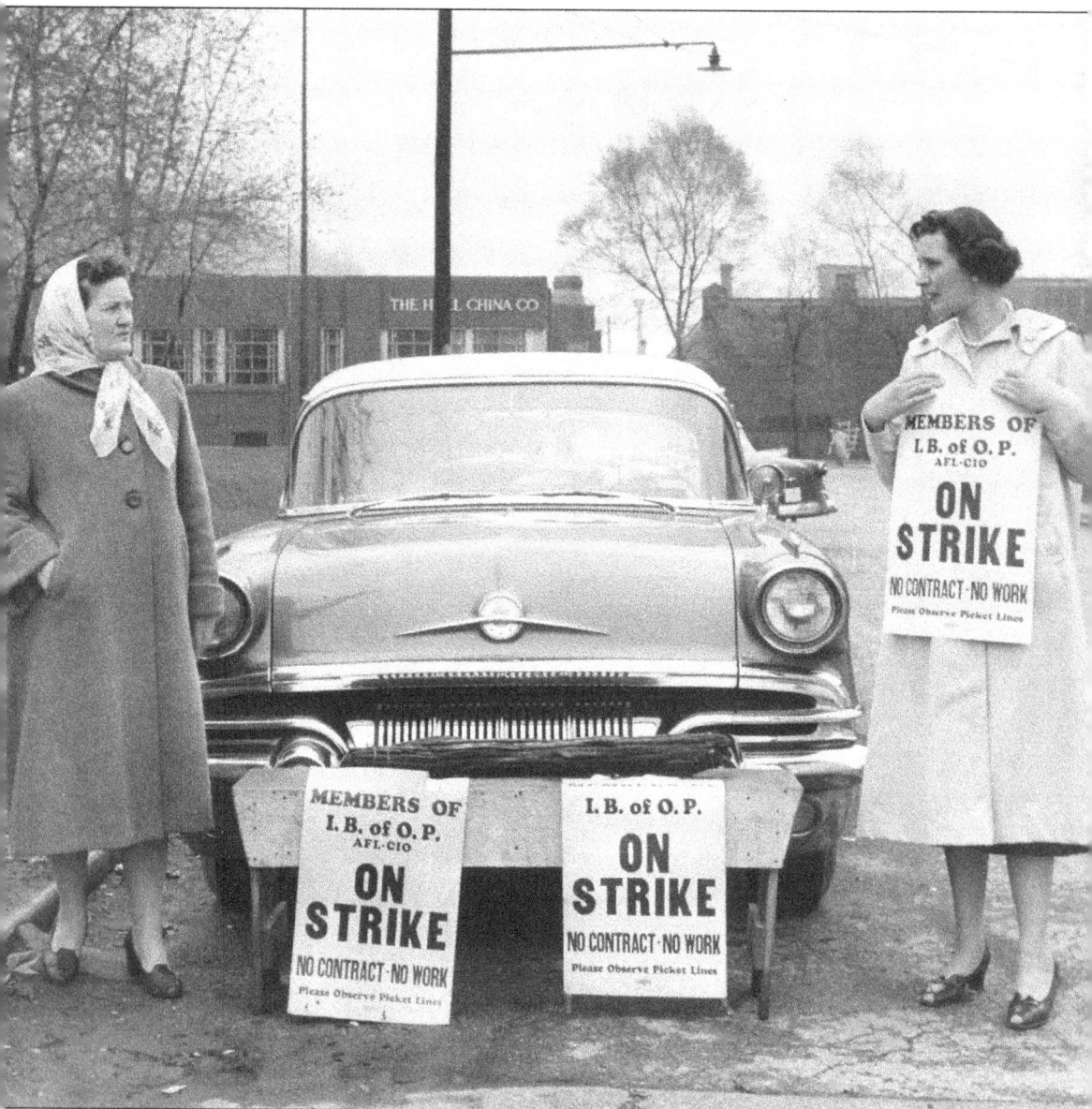

WORKING THE PICKET LINE AT HALL CHINA COMPANY IN 1956. The National Brotherhood of Operative Potters, part of the American Federation of Labor, is composed of unions representing workers in the various ceramic specialties. Notable strikes before 1925 included a work stoppage in 1882, a strike in 1894, and a walkout in 1922. Tariff issues created tensions during the 1870s, and some individual potters created cooperative plants of strikers to remain working. Before the turn of the century, there was a great demand for the thrower. As with any industry, when the economy was good and the demand for goods expanded, skilled tradespeople were difficult to find. In times of recession and depression, the works reduced production or closed. When the use of machinery expanded, many jobs were eliminated. The economic downturn of the 1920s and the Depression led to hard times for all workers in the Ohio Valley. (Cleveland Press Archive, Special Collections, Cleveland State University Library.)

THE DIAMOND, C. 1907. This hub of East Liverpool is listed on the National Register of Historic Places, a reminder of the bustling city center that transferred workers and visitors to Chester, Wellsville, and Newell. (Museum of Ceramics.)

THE BUSINESS CENTER, C. 1910. Trolleys allowed passengers to connect to Wellsville and Chester to ride the train to any part of the United States. (Museum of Ceramics.)

MURPHY & ERLANGER, C. 1909. Potters made fair wages and could afford services and luxuries. Itinerant potters would stay in downtown hotels and shower and shave at the local barbers. Visitors from neighboring cities claimed potters were the best-dressed people in town. (Museum of Ceramics.)

Brunt's Fire, c. 1900–1914. Damage by fire was rarely covered in full. Pottery companies had to accumulate capital to rebuild or close their doors. (Museum of Ceramics.)

EAST LIVERPOOL FIRE DEPARTMENT, C. 1917. The city owned state-of-the-art firefighting equipment. A fire in one part of the downtown could destroy blocks of buildings. A firecrew surveys the damage at the Potters' Mining and Milling Company. (Museum of Ceramics.)

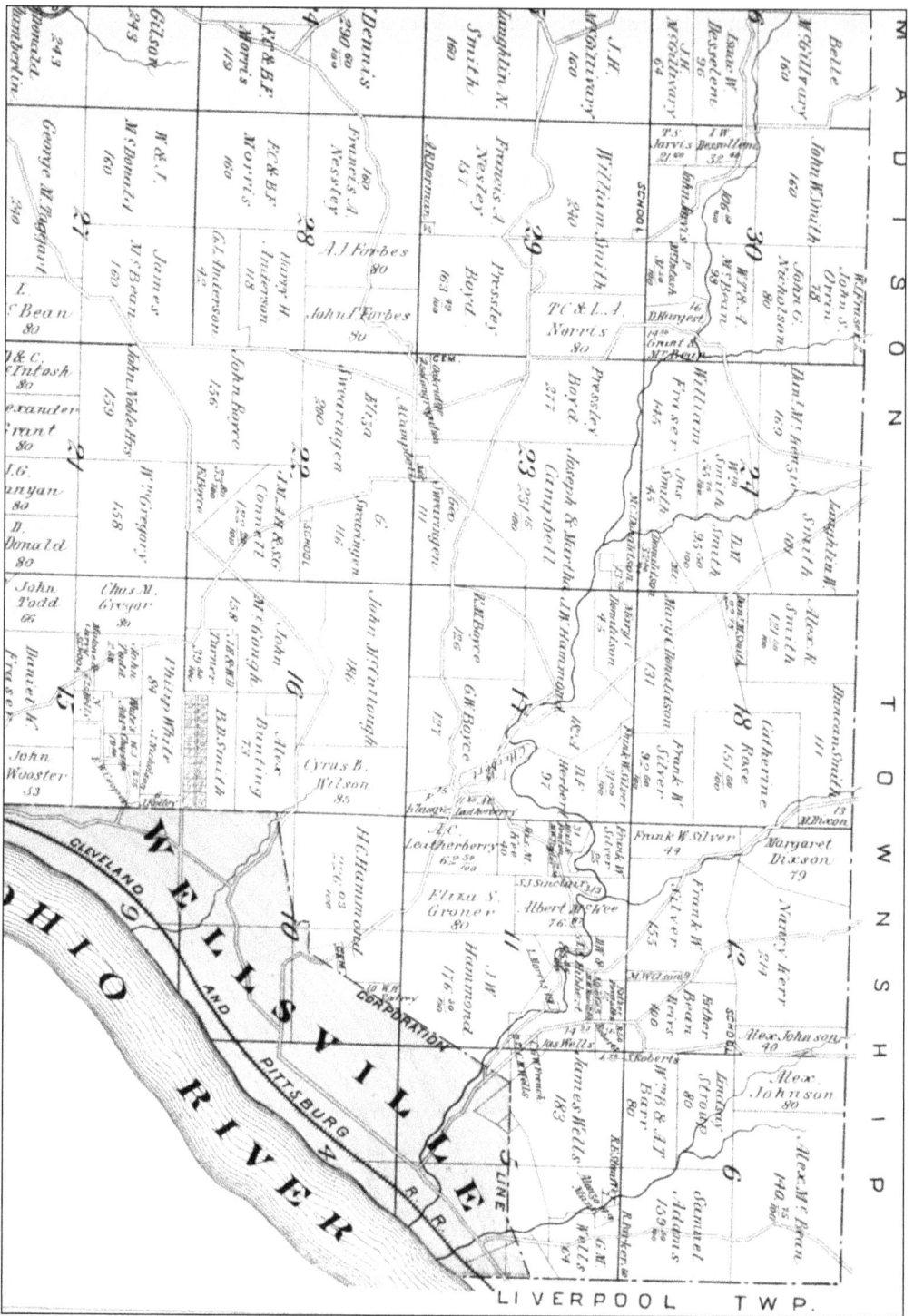

WELLSVILLE, C. 1870.

Three

WELLSVILLE
OHIO

AERIAL VIEW WELLSVILLE, C. 1908. William and Ann Clark Wells built a log house near the mouth of Little Yellow Creek in 1796 and became the first permanent white settlers of what would become a thriving frontier town. Their small home was used as the courthouse from 1798 until 1803, and as a sanctuary for a church visited by a circuit-riding Methodist minister. In 1803, a "Scotch Settlement" was established by Europeans looking for new economic opportunities. The town was platted in 1823 by William Wells, and between that year and 1852, the village grew to be a town, complete with an opera house, a railroad, and a river transportation network. It was later claimed that many houses in the town were stations along the route of the Underground Railroad, which operated as safe havens for blacks escaping slavery. Foundries, sewer works, car shops, potteries, neon signs, and machine and pattern works were major industries. The first pottery company was founded in the town by John Kountz in 1817. The second works was founded in 1826 by Joseph Wells, son of the town founder. The pottery and bricks manufactured in large numbers, combined with the vast transportation network, allowed Wellsville to claim the title as the "Hub of the Pottery and Brick Industry."

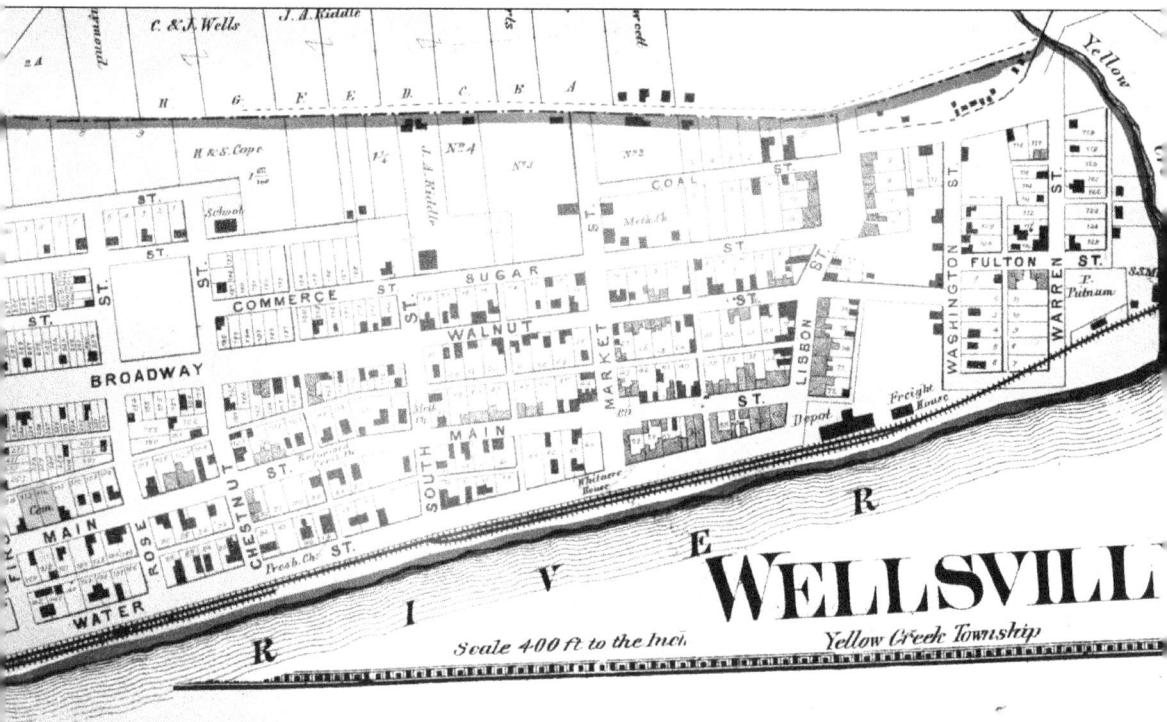

MAIN STREET, C. 1907.

WELLSVILLE DEPOT, C. 1890. Wellsville was the transportation hub of the tri-state area.

MONROE PATTERSON, C. 1922. Patterson arrived in East Liverpool as a child in 1871. He started a small machine shop and foundry that bought out the A.J. Boyce firm in 1898, and was incorporated as the Patterson Foundry and Machine Company the next year. Patterson then went on to serve as treasurer and general manager of the East Liverpool Pottery Company (a precursor to the Hall China Company), in addition to founding the Wellsville China Company. He is well-known for his philanthrophy, having donated playing fields and a medical facility to the area. (Museum of Ceramics.)

WELLSVILLE COMMEMORATIVE PLATE. Herbert Bar, originally of Munich, Germany, designed the Wellville China plate. John Stanway, formerly of England, completed the engraving. Both Bar and Stanway were residents of Wellsville in 1950. (Gray Collection.)

WELLSVILLE CHINA COMPANY, BEFORE THE DELUGE. The Wellsville China Company was located at Ninth and Commercial Streets. The works opened as Morely and Company in 1875 and quickly went through ownership changes, as was common with pottery corporations of the time. (Museum of Ceramics.)

WELLSVILLE CHINA COMPANY DURING THE FLOOD, 1936. High water and floods customarily ran down Third Street across to Commerce and all streets parallel to 18th Street, but in 1936 the flood waters covered the entire section of town. (Museum of Ceramics.)

WELLSVILLE CHINA COMPANY, AUGUST 5, 1921. The employees of the bisque warehouse of Wellsville China are pictured, from left to right, as follows: Rose Bowers, unidentified, unidentified, Tillie Kinds, Emma Kinds, Mary Baker, Lillie Hancock, ? Cane, unidentified, and Mary Streets. Wellsville was purchased by the Sterling China Company in 1970, but was sold to investors several years later. The operations ceased soon after that sale. (Museum of Ceramics.)

ACME CRAFTWARE, AUGUST, 1959. Acme was a large manufacturer of novelty ware. It began as a two-person works and enlarged to operate from this two-story building by the 1950s. The works closed to make way for the new interstate built in the 1960s. (Museum of Ceramics.)

LOADING THE KILN AT ACME, C. 1959. The beehive kiln is loaded the same way as it has been for years. (Museum of Ceramics.)

MODERN KILNS, STERLING CHINA COMPANY, C. 1962, 2002. Mechanization of plants with tunnel kilns began in the 1920s, replacing the elaborate firing ritual of the beehive or milk bottle kilns. Makers who could not compete with firms that installed the new equipment soon closed their doors or were absorbed into other companies. Today, the Sterling works employs over 400 workers and focuses on custom design work for the restaurant and hotel trade. Fourth-generation family members direct day-to-day operations for the company. (Top photo courtesy of Sterling China Company; bottom photo courtesy of Gray Gollection.)

RAILROAD SHOPS. The C & P Railroad provided transportation of pottery goods to markets. The railroad shops helped develop the west end of town, especially on Main Street between 13th and 19th Streets. A hotel catering almost exclusively to railroad workers and their families was built in this neighborhood. Over 100 men were employed at the car shops until the shops were demolished in 1954. Pennsylvania Railroad freight trains continued to run along these tracks until the railroad was dissolved in the Penn Central merger of 1968. (Gray Collection.)

THE WHITACRE HOUSE HOTEL. January 27, 1857, marked the opening of the American Hotel on the corner of Water (later Riverside) and Market (Fourth) Streets. T.W. Whitacre was the proprietor of the National House Hotel on Main and Lisbon (Third) Streets. He remodeled his new hotel to be one of the best in the region. Major businesses, federal officials including Lewis B. Cass (then U.S. Secretary of State), and later presidents Andrew Johnson and James A. Garfield were all guests at the hotel. The most infamous visitor was Confederate General John Hunt Morgan, who was held prisoner at "The Whitacre" in 1863. Abraham Lincoln stopped at the hotel on his way to his first inauguration in 1861. (Gray Collection.)

THE FIRST WELLSVILLE FAIR, 1889. The first fair was held in 1889 at the grounds at Fifteenth and Commerce Streets. The main grandstands were located on Commerce, while the animal stables were on present-day Maple Avenue. The racetrack extended as far as Aten Avenue. By the mid-1890s, lots were sold and houses were constructed in the former fairgrounds area. At the turn of the century, a path for Clark Avenue was surveyed and additional lots were sold during a successful marketing campaign in 1903. (Gray Collection)

J.C. LAWSON'S 5 & 10, C. 1949. The Lawson Family has been involved in business since 1841. The general store, shown as the five-and-dime in this photograph from 1950, was first established in 1903. (Gray Collection)

JOHNNIE'S LUNCH, C. 1950. Wellsville-born-and-raised John Albaneso opened Johnnie's Student Confectionary in 1938 on Center Street. He purchased Grafton's Wimpy's Restaurant on Main a year later and relocated his business. After serving in World War II, Albaneso reopened his restaurant. He moved again in the early 1970s and reopened as Johnnie's Lunch. The establishment was a long-time employer of local high school students and was a favorite hangout for students in the 1950s. (Gray Collection.)

CENTRAL FEDERAL SAVINGS, C. 1950. The Central Building and Loan was first organized in 1892 in a small second-floor room over the McIntosh Drug Store on the corner of Ninth and Main Streets. Officers in that year included: John S. Smith, president; J.W. Russell, vice president; Mary L. Smith, secretary; A.G. McKenzie, treasurer; and P.M. Smith, attorney. (Gray Collection.)

71

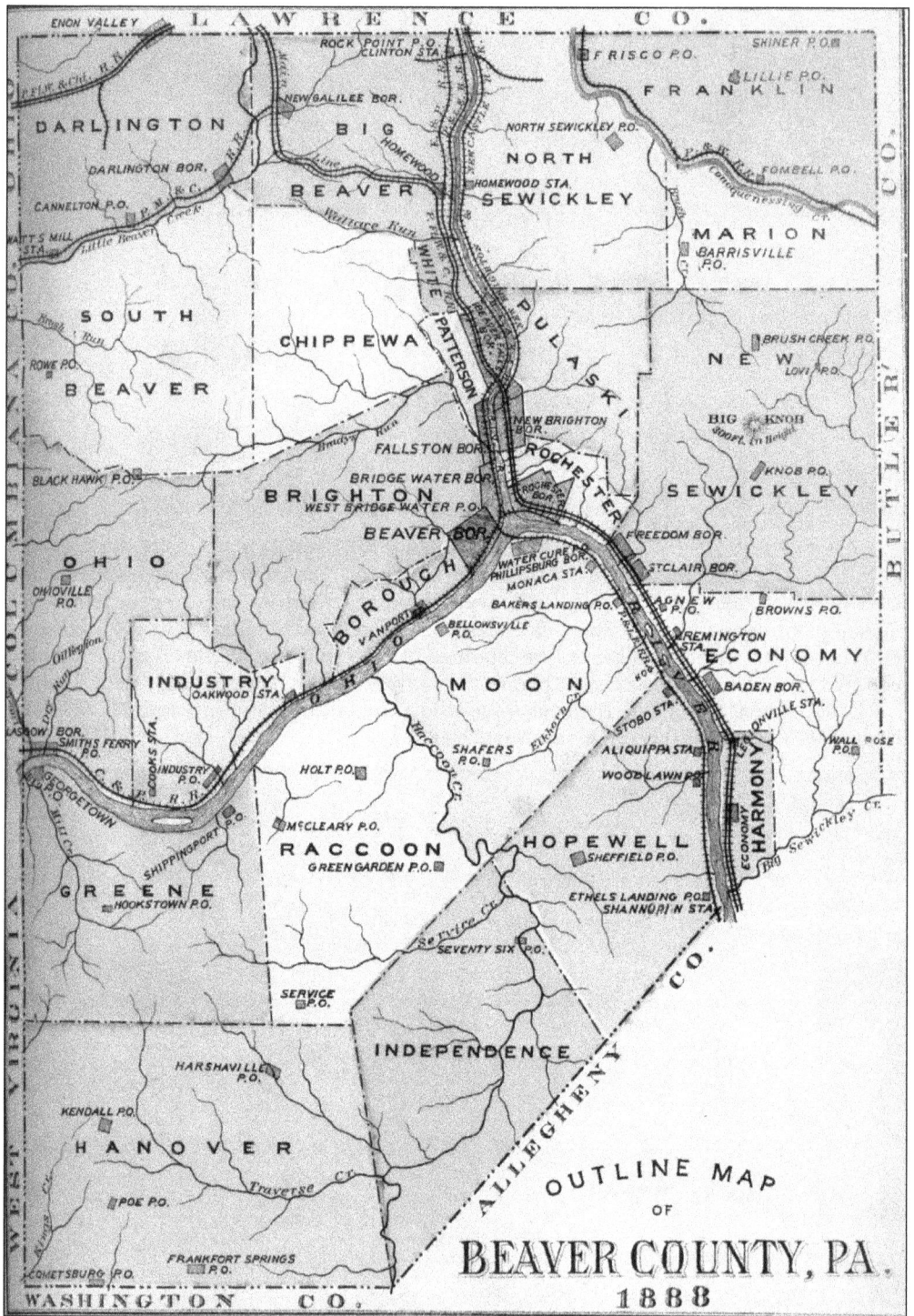

ENON VALLEY

ROCK POINT P.O.
CLINTON STA.

SHINER P.O.

F RISCO P.O.

LILLIE P.O.

F R A N K L I N

P.F.W. & CH. R.R.

NEW GALILEE BOR.

NORTH SEWICKLEY P.O.

D A R L I N G T O N

B I G

N O R T H
S E W I C K L E Y

FOMBELL P.O.

DARLINGTON BOR.

HOMEWOOD STA.

HOMEWOOD

M A R I O N

CANNELTON P.O.

B E A V E R

P.R.C.

BARRISVILLE
P.O.

WATT'S MILL STA.

Little Beaver Creek

Wallace Run

S O U T H

ROWE P.O.

C H I P P E W A

N E W

BRUSH CREEK P.O.

LOVI P.O.

B E A V E R

BLACK HAWK P.O.

Brady Run

NEW BRIGHTON BOR.

BIG
KNOB

KNOB P.O.

FALLSTON BOR.

R O C H E S T E R

S E W I C K L E Y

B R I G H T O N

BRIDGE WATER BOR.
WEST BRIDGE WATER P.O.

ROCH. BOR.

FREEDOM BOR.

O H I O

OHIOVILLE
P.O.

BEAVER BOR.

WATER CURE CO.
PHILLIPSBURG BOR.
MONACA STA.

ST CLAIR BOR.

B O R O U G H

VANPORT

BAKERS LANDING P.O.

AGNEW
P.O.

BROWNS P.O.

Ohioview

BELLOWSVILLE
P.O.

REMINGTON
STA.

E C O N O M Y

I N D U S T R Y

O H I O

OAKWOOD STA.

M O O N

BADEN BOR.

SMITHS FERRY
P.O.

INDUSTRY
P.O.

C.P.C. & ST.L. R.R.

SHAFERS
P.O.

STOBO STA.

ALIQUIPPA STA.

WALL ROSE
P.O.

GEORGETOWN

HOLT P.O.

WOODLAWN P.O.

SHIPPINGPORT P.O.

McCLEARY P.O.

R A C C O O N

H O P E W E L L

ECONOMY
H A R M O N Y

G R E E N E

GREEN GARDEN P.O.

SHEFFIELD P.O.

HOOKSTOWN P.O.

ETHELS LANDING P.O.
SHANNOPIN STA.

SEVENTY SIX P.O.

SERVICE
P.O.

I N D E P E N D E N C E

HARSHAVILLE
P.O.

KENDALL P.O.

H A N O V E R

POE P.O.

OUTLINE MAP

OF

COMETSBURG P.O.

FRANKFORT SPRINGS
P.O.

BEAVER COUNTY, PA.

1888

BEAVER, C. 1880.

Three

BEAVER AREA
PENNSYLVANIA

View on the Beaver River, showing the Hills of Beaver County.

BEAVER AREA, C. 1890. Thomas Mifflin authorized Daniel Leet on September 28, 1791 to survey near the mouth of the Beaver River. Fort McIntosh had long been established in the area. French and Native Americans had maintained prior permanent settlements, but the survey involved 200 acres of town lots, 1,000 acres of "outlots", and 500 acres of land for the creation of an academy. On March 12, 1800, the town of Beaver was designated as the county seat, and it was incorporated two years later.

It is impossible to accurately list all of the individuals producing pottery in the Beaver area, but key geographic areas of production are known. Villages were used as identification stamps and stencils on ware because the larger towns were familiar to river travelers. The one-kiln works were frequently not located in the town itself, but were situated near clay deposits. These were close enough to ship the goods by wagon to river transportation. Thirteen potters are listed in the Beaver County census of 1850. Makers from this early time period include N.J. Lloyd, C. Kelin, and Harbaugh. (Museum of Ceramics.)

BEAVER AREA, C. 1890. Bridges linking Beaver Falls to New Brighton included a covered bridge, which was demolished in 1900. The Pennsylvania Railroad Bridge is seen in the middle. The Tenth Street Bridge, opened by the Penn Bridge Company around 1900 for trolley and pedestrian crossing, is in the distance. The canal runs along the right bank of the Beaver River. (Beaver Falls Historical Society.)

THE SANDY AND BEAVER CANAL. The Sandy and Beaver Canal Company was incorporated in January 1826 and amended in 1830, but work was not begun until winter 1834. Canal proponents pushed for expansion into Beaver and surrounding areas, but natural disasters, railroad competition, and financial mismanagement resulted in the end of the canal system six years later. (The Museum of Ceramics.)

DRY GOODS ADVERTISEMENT. Although people purchased wares directly from the local pottery, dry goods merchants also frequently carried pottery and crockery. This advertisement from Beaver Falls features "Queensware." (Allen County Public Library.)

THE RUSSELL WORKS/VANPORT BRIDGE. *Caldwell's Centennial Atlas* shows the Russell pottery in Boro Township in 1876. Russell produced crockery from around 1847 until the 1890s. Ralph Russell began the business and his son Albert carried on, producing hand-turned stoneware products. Records show that John Weaver produced crockery in the Beaver area from 1855 until around 1895. George, John's son, worked with him to produce the blue slip decorated items. Flowers and trees were used as decorations. Pottery from this firm is impressed "J. Weaver." Construction of a new route for state highway 60 and a new Vanport Bridge have erased all evidence of the early pottery industry. (Allen County Public Library)

75

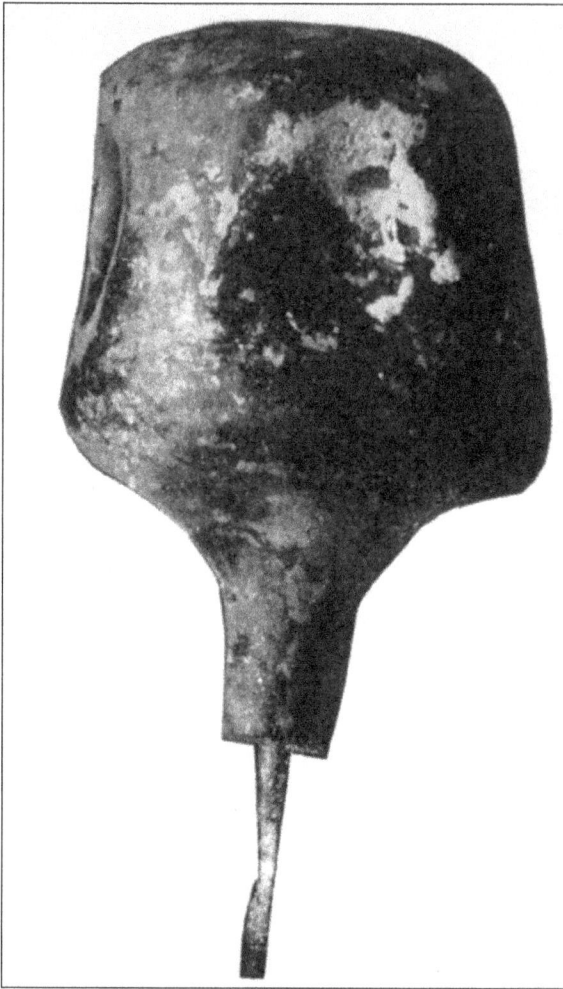

EARLY SLIP DECORATED POTTERY TOOLS. Early salt-glazed and yellow ware were decorated with these tools, including the quill decorator above. The Johnson Brothers began production some time around 1850. Floral slip decorated and blue stenciled trademark made their wares easy to identify. Thomas McKenzie and J. McKenzie partnered in the early 1860s to create pieces with freehand decorations. Flowers and portraits are featured in their unusual designs. The firm produced decorative ware for only a few years. (Allen County Public Library.)

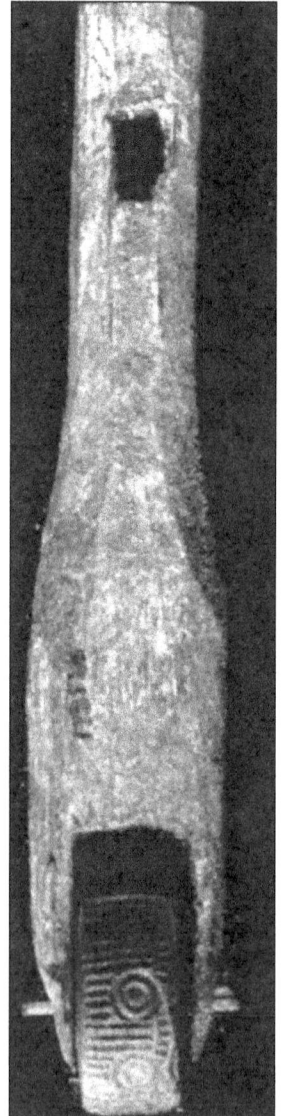

BEAVER FALLS, c. 1890. Beaver Falls Art Tile, known for their custom design and fine worksmanship, and Mayer China Company, noted for their commercial dinnerware production, significantly bolstered the economy of the region. (Beaver Falls Historical Society.)

BROOME DESIGNED ART TILES. Noted designer Isaac Broome worked at the Beaver Falls Art Tile Company. His tiles are highly collectible today and can be seen on display at the Beaver Historical Museum. (Beaver County Historical Museum.)

BEAVER FALLS TILE COMPANY. (Beaver Falls Historical Society.)

MAYER CHINA COMPANY. The Mayer China works was located on the Beaver River. Founded in 1881 by brothers Joseph and Earnest Mayer, the river location allowed convenient transportation of supplies and finished wares. The Mayers purchased a factory run by the Economites, an early sect occupying Beaver Valley. The brothers were front runners in developing a modern factory, installing tunnel kilns in the pioneer stages of development. (Beaver Falls Historical Society.)

LINING DEPARTMENT, MAYER CHINA. Mayer underglazed the ware before glazing to insure the pattern would stay clear. Their slogan was "The Ware With the Wear-Resisting Glaze." (Museum of Ceramics.)

SPRAY GLAZING MACHINE AT MAYER, C. 1947.

THE AUTOMATIC JIGGER, MAYER CHINA, C. 1949.

BEAVER FALLS, SEVENTH STREET, C. 1907.

SHENANGO OPERATIONS AT THE MAYER PLANT. The Mayer Family continued to operate the company until 1964 when Shenango Ceramics of New Castle assumed ownership. The Interpace Corporation took over in 1968 and a shift was made from dinnerware and commercial ware to building products. The Rifenburgh Family purchased the company and operated under the Mayer China name until 1984, when Syracuse China Corporation of New York purchased the trademark. Today, Brighton Falls China Company produces the lines of the former Mayer Company, but Syracuse (now owned by Libbey, Inc. of Toledo, Ohio) retains the Mayer China name. Operating from the former Mayer plant located on the Beaver River, Brighton Falls China produces ware for commercial uses, including use by casinos and hotels. They also offer custom design work for the small restauranteur. (Cleveland Press Archive, Special Collections, Cleveland State University Library.)

BEAVER COLLEGE

—AND—

MUSICAL INSTITUTE,

The only Institution chartered by the State in the county, and the only one that has any authority to grant diplomas.

Its Sessions open middle of September and first of January and April.

One of the Largest and most Flourishing Ladies' Schools in the Country.

English, Classical, Musical and College Preparatory Courses provided, and last instruction in

DRAWING AND PAINTING.

Natural Sciences illustrated by the use of Apparatus, Maps, Charts and Cabinet.

A FINE READING ROOM & LIBRARY

Open for the use of the Pupils.

Persons beginning in Vocal and Instrumental Music and Voice Culture, receive lessons daily without additional charge. Boarding pupils are in the family of the President.

Prices have been Greatly Reduced for Board, Music and Tuition, SEND FOR CATALOGUE TO THE PRESIDENT,

REV. R. T. TAYLOR, Beaver, Pa.

CITY DIRECTORY ADVERTISEMENT, BEAVER COLLEGE. The organization changed their name to Arcadia University in 2001. (Allen County Public Library.)

BEAVER COLLEGE MUSIC INSTITUTE, C. 1914. This is an informal portrait of the graduating class. Founded as a small women's college in 1853, it relocated closer to Philadelphia nearly 75 years ago. (Forney Collection.)

BEAVER COLLEGE MUSIC INSTITUTE, C. 1914. This is a formal portrait of the graduating class. The college first opened with a liberal arts curriculum but soon expanded to include music, art, and science departments. (Forney Collection.)

View of Chester, W. Va.

CHESTER, WEST VIRGINIA, C. 1909.

Five

CHESTER
WEST VIRGINIA

CHESTER, C. 1913. Chester was laid out in 1896 and incorporated in 1907 by J.E. McDonald. The name was purportedly chosen because it was short and easily remembered. Early residents worked in the pottery industry, and as land became scarce in nearby East Liverpool, pottery works relocated in the town. Home to Rock Springs Park, the area received thousands of weekend visitors intent on picnicing, swimming, and riding the scenic railway, the chute, and merry-go-round.

SUSPENSION BRIDGE. Bridges were a critical component of the development of the town of Chester. Workers could quickly travel to the new factories on the other side of the Ohio River and fun-seekers no longer had to rely on ferry transportation to visit Rock Springs Park. Work began on the suspension bridge in 1895. It opened to the public two years later. (Gray Collection.)

DECORATING ROOM, C. 1910.

HARKER POTTERY COMPANY. This publicity photo of the decorating room at Harker Pottery was taken for postcard confirmation of orders sent to wholesale buyers. The factory required renovation in 1931, and the decision was made to relocate from East Liverpool to higher grounds across the river in Chester. At the height of production in 1965, the works employed 300 workers who turned out 25 million pieces of dinnerware each year. (Museum of Ceramics.)

HARKER POTTERY COMPANY, C. 1940S.

HARKER KILNS, OCTOBER, 1957. When the factory was moved from East Liverpool to Chester, these kilns were left to the elements. (Museum of Ceramics.)

LADIES' REST HOUSE, ROCK SPRINGS PARK, C. 1890S. (Museum of Ceramics.)

SCENIC RAILROAD AND CHUTE, ROCK SPRINGS PARK. Jim McDonald opened Rock Springs Park in 1898. Two years later C.A. Smith purchased the grounds and added the hand-carved merry-go-round. (Gray Collection.)

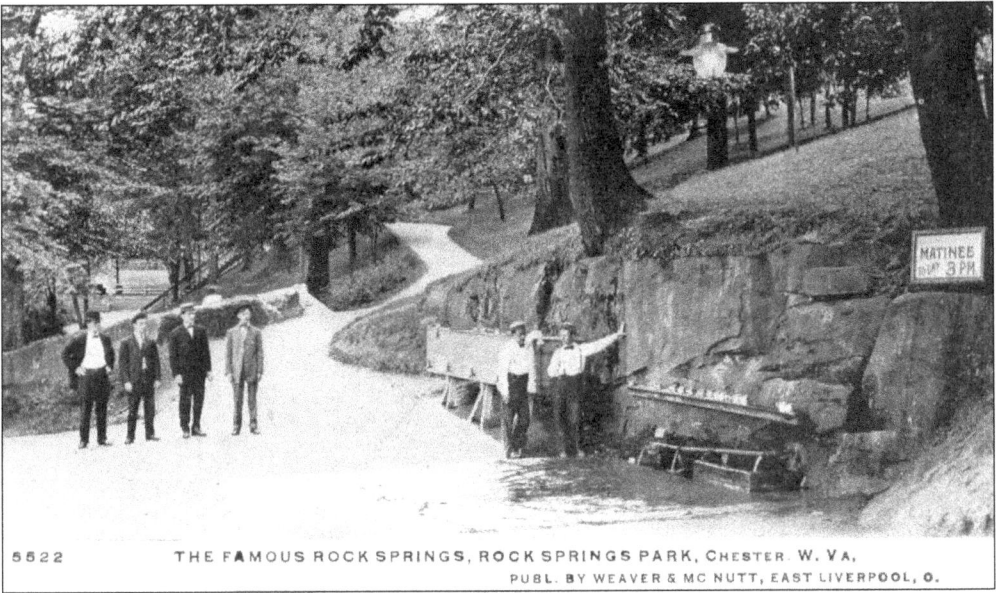

THE SPRINGS, ROCK SPRINGS PARK. Before the advent of paper cups, those wishing to drink the fresh water used the tin cups at the spring. (Museum of Ceramics.)

FLOWER GARDENS, ROCK SPRINGS PARK. The park grounds were frequently used as picnic facilities. Weekends sometimes drew as many as 20,000 visitors. (Museum of Ceramics.)

THE SWIMMING POOL, ROCK SPRINGS PARK. Changing rooms were housed inside the swimming pavilion. The park continued to operate until the late 1960s. By the 1970s, it was demolished to make way for highway construction. (Museum of Ceramics.)

THE PAVILION, ROCK SPRINGS PARK. Dancing, musical performances, and speeches were held in the pavilion. The presence of the pottery industry can be seen in the smoking kilns in the distance, on the East Liverpool side of the banks of the Ohio River. (Gray Collection.)

WATERFORD RACE TRACK. At the turn of the century, horseracing and sleigh riding competitions took place from the Pennsylvania Railroad tracks at the foot of Jefferson Street to the lower end of Broadway in East Palestine. When the city council voted to prohibit racing in town, a mock funeral procession was held along the route and citizens came to the Waterford Track to see it. (Gray Collection.)

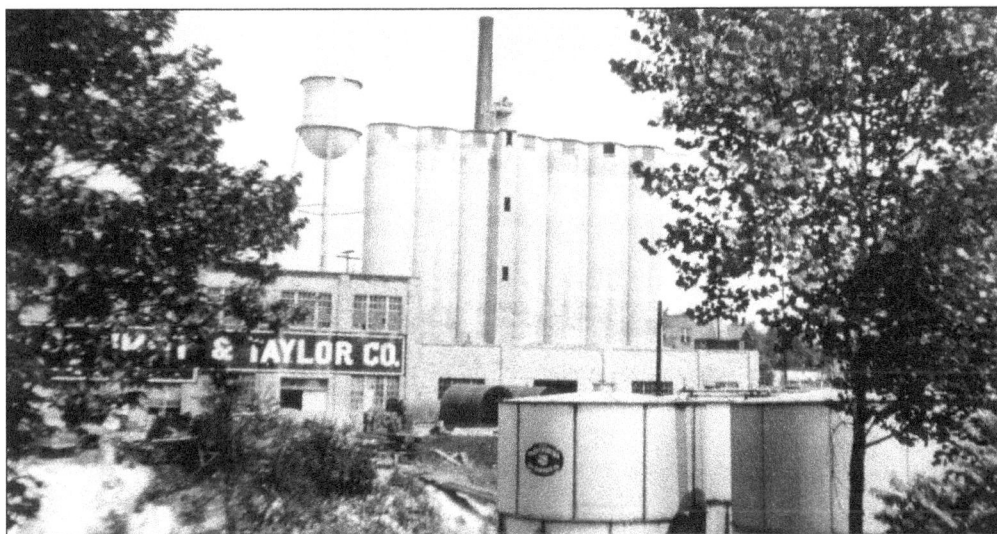

TAYLOR, SMITH & TAYLOR. John Taylor was president of Knowles, Taylor and Knowles in addition to serving as Knowles, Taylor and Anderson Company (later known as the Potters' Supply Company). In his spare time he served as postmaster of East Liverpool, beginning in 1864. In 1892, Taylor was appointed to the rank of colonel by Governor McKinley. T.S.&T. was purchased by the Anchor Hocking Corporation in 1973. At that time the company manufactured earthenware (ironstone), fine stoneware, institutional china dinnerware, and commemorative collector plates. By September 30, 1987, with less than 250 employees, Anchor Hocking, in a move for a fiscal reorganization, closed T.S.&T. citing an inability to keep pace with the low import pieces of foreign competitors. (Museum of Ceramics.)

Newell, West Virginia, c. 1890.

Six

NEWELL

WEST VIRGINIA

NEWELL, C. 1900. After years of fighting between Native Americans and white settlers, Jacob Nessly and William Hamilton established homes and businesses in the Newell area. Early industries included farming, orcharding, and coopersmithing. John Newell of Pughtown purchased farm land in 1837, and John's son, Hugh, laid out and sold land to new settlers where the present town stands in the 1850s. The first pottery was established by Curtis and James Larkins and William Thompson in the 1850s. The yellow ware producing kiln was located about 300 yards below the end of the present-day Newell Bridge. Production continued until the late 1870s when economic conditions forced its closure.

Newell continued as a farm area and ferry terminus to Jethrow Hollow until 1891, when a group of investors purchased large tracts of land to develop housing for the workers of nearby East Liverpool. A Pittsburgh syndicate failed in this attempt, but later the North American Manufacturing Company, a group of local investors, were successful in developing the land. Housing, combined with bridge transportation over the Ohio River, expanded population from 130 residents to just under 800 by 1907.

THE NEWELL BRIDGE. A bridge was necessary to move pottery workers across the river in both directions. The North American Manufacturing Company controlled the Newell Bridge Company, which charged a toll to cross. Completion on July 4, 1905, meant an intense period of building for the town of Newell. (Museum of Ceramics.)

EDWIN M. KNOWLES CHINA COMPANY. Edwin S. Knowles China Company opened in 1905 and closed in 1963. The company would benefit from the new bridges completed right after the turn of the century. By 1906, the company added extra kiln capacity and workers. (Museum of Ceramics.)

RESIDENCES OF E.M. KNOWLES (ABOVE) AND W.E WELLS (BELOW). Newell offered attractive hillside home lots. New bridge construction meant travel to work took only a few short minutes. E.M. Knowles and W.E. Wells both built mansions in the new subdivision. (Museum of Ceramics.)

EDWIN M. KNOWLES CHINA COMPANY BASEBALL TEAM. The china company had several teams. The players pictured above are members of "Team One".Competition between other potteries, factories, and city teams was fierce and was covered by the local newspapers. The team featured many players who would later compete on professional teams. Curtis Welsh played for the St. Louis Browns, George Carely played for the Baltimore Orioles, and Alfred Shaw and John Goodwin joined the Boston Red Sox. (Museum of Ceramics.)

THE LAUGHLIN BROTHERS POTTERY. The Laughlin Brothers, Homer and Stephen, founded their company in 1871 on Little Beaver Creek, a few miles from East Liverpool. In 1872, they collected a bonus from the city after they established a pottery that produced white ware to compete against imported crockery. HLCC began in 1874 as the "Ohio Valley Pottery." Two years later the "Laughlin Brothers" won top awards for white ware at the Centennial Exposition in Philadelphia. (Los Angeles Public Library.)

HOMER LAUGHLIN CHINA COMPANY, NEWELL. Homer Laughlin retired to California in 1897 and the remaining partners began a series of plant expansions. The original works was traded for a facility in the East End, but demand was high and the firm had little room to make the necessary plant enlargements. The company purchased a three-mile tract of land in Newell and opened their new plant in 1907. (Allen County Public Library.)

THE NEW

FIESTA

FIESTA ACCESSORIES, 1997. Modeling the succesful design of the original Fiestaware, "New Fiesta" introduced color-cordinated accessories in 1997.

Opposite: **FIESTAWARE.** HLCC formed the North American Manufacturing Company that would eventually develop ten acres on the site of the former Larkins Pottery. An additional 100-acre park adjoined the works with formal gardens, a baseball park, a zoo, and an outdoor theater. At its peak, HLCC employed 3,500 people and operated at five different plants in Newell.

Frederick Hurten Rhead was hired as art director of Homer Laughlin China in 1927. Rhead's Fiestaware design was introduced in 1935, and in 1959 Fiesta Ironstone replaced the original Fiesta. Production halted entirely in 1973. Celebration of Fiesta's centennial in 1986 lead to a "New Fiesta" with all-new lead-free glazes. New glazes continue to be introduced each year, with production of commercial restaurant Fiestware offered in additional colors. Today, the factory is one of the country's largest china manufacturers. A fourth generation of the Wells family continues to operate the company. New products include the plum color introduced in 2002. (Courtesy of the Homer Laughlin China Company.)

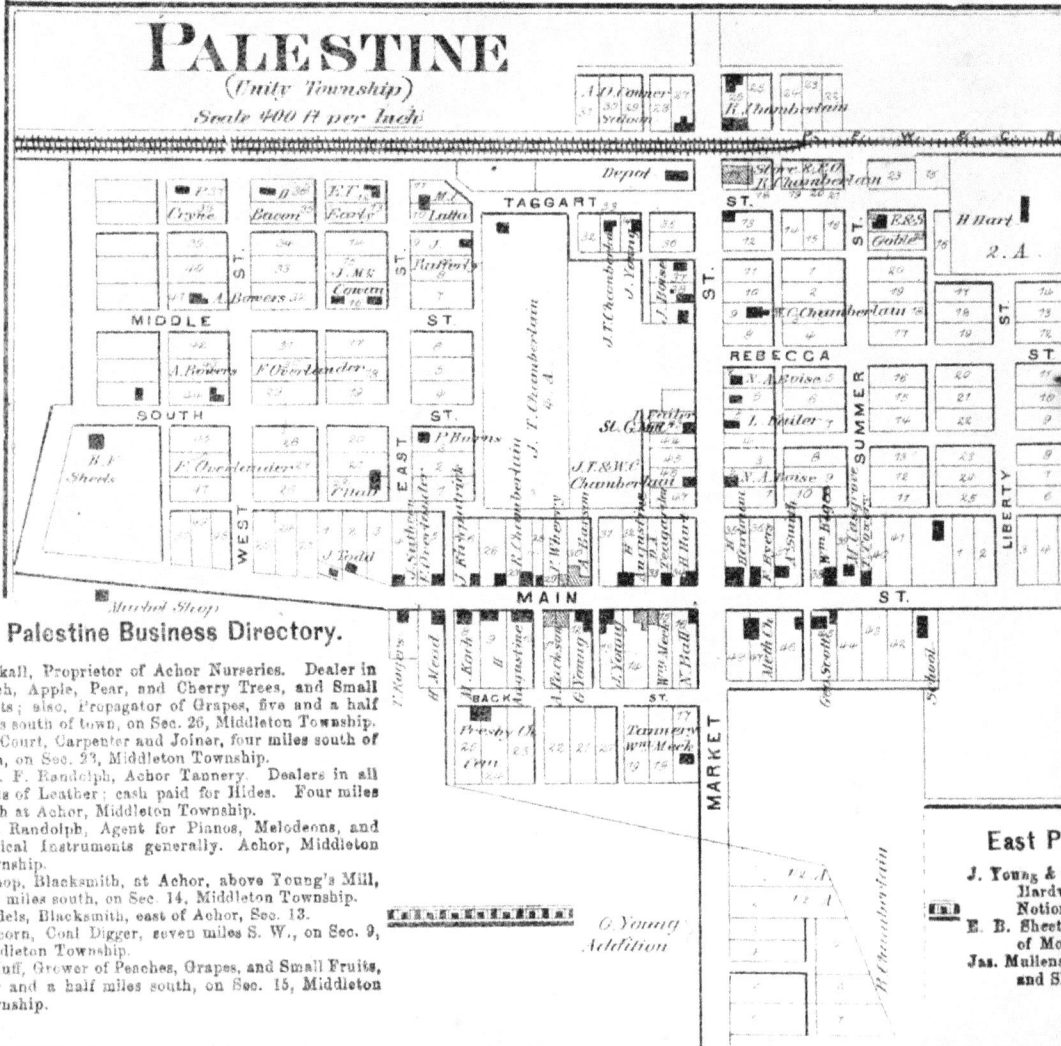

PALESTINE
(Unity Township)
Scale 400 ft per Inch

East Palestine Business Directory.

G. H. Mackall, Proprietor of Achor Nurseries. Dealer in Peach, Apple, Pear, and Cherry Trees, and Small Fruits; also, Propagator of Grapes, five and a half miles south of town, on Sec. 26, Middleton Township.

Frederick Court, Carpenter and Joiner, four miles south of town, on Sec. 23, Middleton Township.

B. F. & J. F. Randolph, Achor Tannery. Dealers in all kinds of Leather; cash paid for Hides. Four miles south at Achor, Middleton Township.

E. L. Fitz Randolph, Agent for Pianos, Melodeons, and Musical Instruments generally. Achor, Middleton Township.

S. R. Bishop, Blacksmith, at Achor, above Young's Mill, four miles south, on Sec. 14, Middleton Township.

Isaac Randels, Blacksmith, east of Achor, Sec. 13.

W. G. Allcorn, Coal Digger, seven miles S. W., on Sec. 9, Middleton Township.

William Huff, Grower of Peaches, Grapes, and Small Fruits, four and a half miles south, on Sec. 15, Middleton Township.

EAST PALESTINE, OHIO, C. 1870.

104

Seven

EAST PALESTINE
OHIO

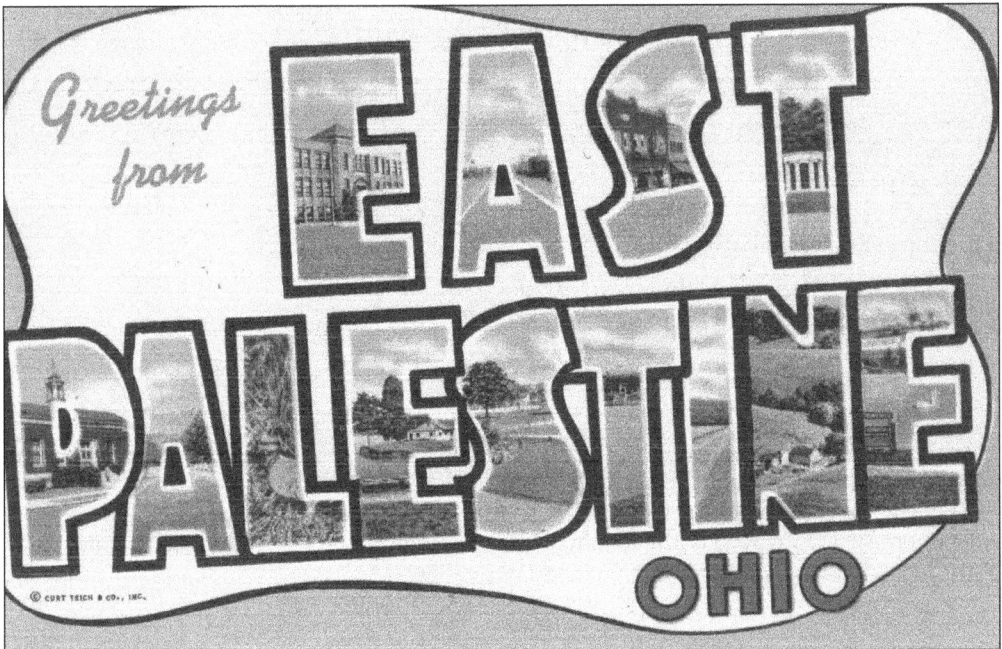

WELCOME TO EAST PALESTINE. Thomas McCalla and William Grate laid out the town of Mechanicsburg in 1828, but East Palestine was officially recognized as the town's name in 1832. An addition was platted by Robert Chamberlain in 1835, and the majority of the present-day town was constructed on this land. The first log cabin was built in 1828 by Grate, and it served as a store for Edward Allender around 1830. Chamberlain also opened a highly successful mercantile around the same time. The town was incorporated in 1875, with the election of officers the following year. East Palestine had a large reserve of natural resources including coal, fire clay, cannel, oil, brick shales, and building stones. The soil was fertile for agriculture and an orchard industry soon developed. Food, steel, furniture, and rubber products, in addition to pottery, were manufactured in the city. (Gray Collection.)

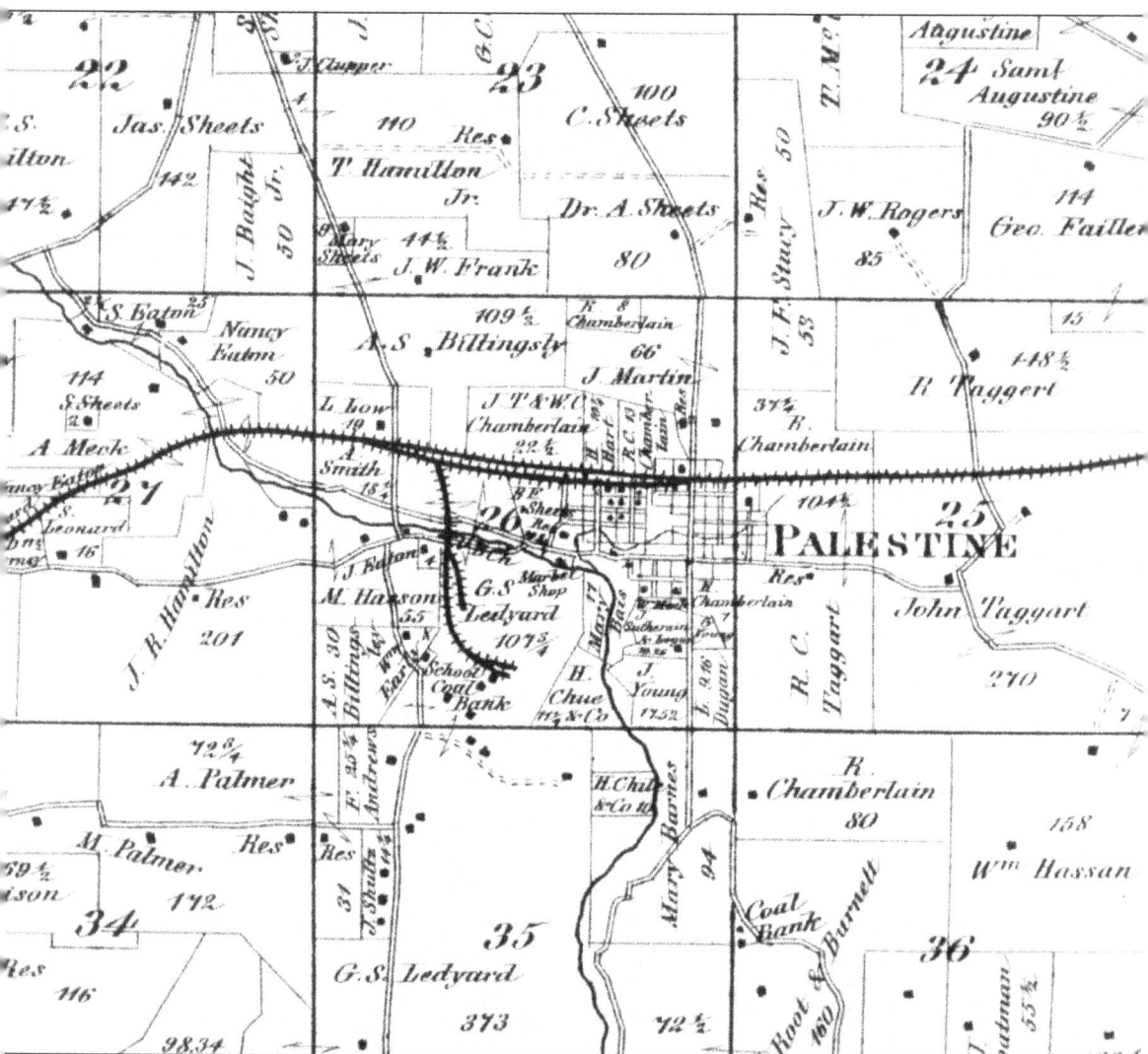

EAST PALESTINE, OHIO, C. 1870. In 1879, East Palestine was called "the largest and most prosperous village in the township, and one of the most flourishing in the county." It boasted a depot on the Fort Wayne Railroad, important coal interests, and a large trade that increased until the end of the decade. (Allen County Public Library.)

MAIN STREET, C. 1962. In 1879, Horace Mack's *History of Columbiana County* reported, "At East Palestine excellent potter's clay has been found and a company is about being formed to establish a pottery to manufacture Rockingham ware." The town mounted an organized campaign to attract a pottery works in 1878. It wasn't until later that year that clay tests incited Herman Feustal and "Mr." Waltz to build works and fire their first kiln in 1880. The ware was given to town residents to celebrate the opening. (Allen County Public Library.)

FEUSTAL POTTERY SITE, C. 1878. East Palestine's first manufacturing company was a 13,800 square foot pottery with three kilns. It was located on land along the Pennsylvania Railroad tracks in the McCalia Addition. (Allen County Public Library.)

Our . .
Specialties
Are . .
Artistic.

The OHIO CHINA CO.
EAST PALESTINE, OHIO.

WE LEAD
. . IN HIGH GRADE

PORCELAIN.

CRACKER JAR

Our . . . .
Decorations
Are . . .
Attractive.

CHOCOLATE POT.

NEW YORK SALESROOM: CHICAGO SALESROOM:

ADVERTISING FOR THE TRADE, C. 1890S. Benjamin Nowling replaced Waltz at Feustal's firm, and when local lumberman James Taggart Chamberlain joined the management in 1882, it became "Feustal, Nowling and Company." Two years later, the partners sold to a group of potters from East Liverpool and the name changed again to the East Palestine Pottery Company. The group enlarged the plant and began manufacturing white and decorated ware.

EPPC. The East Palestine Pottery Company was purchased by a group of town investors in 1889. By 1893, when George and Frank Sebring from East Liverpool arrived to operate the works on a commission arrangement, the company was in poor economic shape and had established a negative reputation for meeting schedules and deliveries. The Sebrings were so successful in reestablishing EPPC that the merchants provided additional land on the eastern side of town in 1896. The new works opened with William Shaw George at the head of the decorating department. The next year, George accepted the manager's role and the company was on the road to a national reputation.

W.S. GEORGE. East Liverpool city directories for 1870 show that the George family engaged in a custom woodworking business. Moving to East Palestine in 1897 to accept a position at the Sebring plant, George took control of the operations just a few years later. He was a noted philanthropist, donating money to the local United Presbyterian Church and the hospital in Abyssinia. He was a trustee of the University of Cairo in Egypt. (Los Angeles Public Library.)

PROMOTING W.S. GEORGE CHINA. W.S. George had purchased controlling interest by 1904 and had built the new "Continental China" works. East Palestine became the company headquarters when Canonsburg (1901) and Kittaning (1905) plants were absorbed into the firm. George brought the first national gas line into the town through Pine Hollow from Negley. (Forney Collection.)

Pattern: "BLUE FLOWER"
Colors: Blue & Grey

Pattern: "PROVINCIAL"
Colors: Earth Brown & Chartreuse

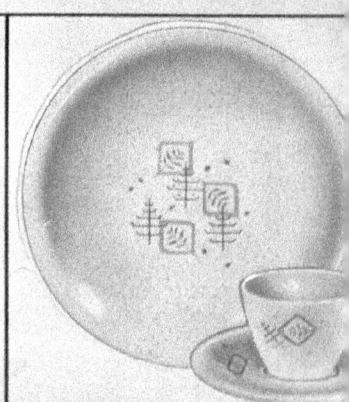

Pattern: "ARBOR"
Colors: Turquoise, Pink & Grey with texture glaze.

W.S. GEORGE POTTERY CATALOG. Catalogs were an important component of the sales strategy at W. S. George. This one was published before the addition of Plant No. 4, in East Palestine on a site next to Plant #1. Cannonsburg and Kittanning, Pennsylvania housed the other plants. Strategic plant location on or near rail lines was an important factor mentioned in their advertising promotions. (Forney Collection.)

PLANT NO. 4, W.S. GEORGE POTTERY, C. 1940. The main offices and first plant at W. S. George were located in East Palestine. Plant No. 4 was built on the site of the original works after a disastrous fire on May 5, 1912 destroyed the "Continental" works. It would take until the fall of 1923 to recoup the loss of the $125,000 plant and for construction to begin on a replacement. (Forney Collection.)

DRAWING THE WARE, W.S. GEORGE, C. 1952. Cavett was W.S. George's mother's middle name and Shaw his father's middle name. Cavett-Shaw was the contemporary dinnerware produced to compete with a large import market and the trend for modern design of the 1950s. (Forney Collection.)

LINING THE PIECE. "Diz" Rupert of W.S. George lines a piece with gold in 1947. (Forney Collection.)

DECORATING DEPARTMENT, W.S. GEORGE, C. 1944. Herb Mohr and Harry Fitzsimmons are at work at the continuous decorating kiln. Ben Anderson supervised production in the department. (Forney Collection.)

THE SALES TEAM OF W.S. GEORGE, C. 1952. (Forney Collection.)

Drawing Decorated Ware at the George Factory, c. 1940s. (Forney Collection.)

Cutting the Pug, c. 1940s, W.S. George. (Forney Collection.)

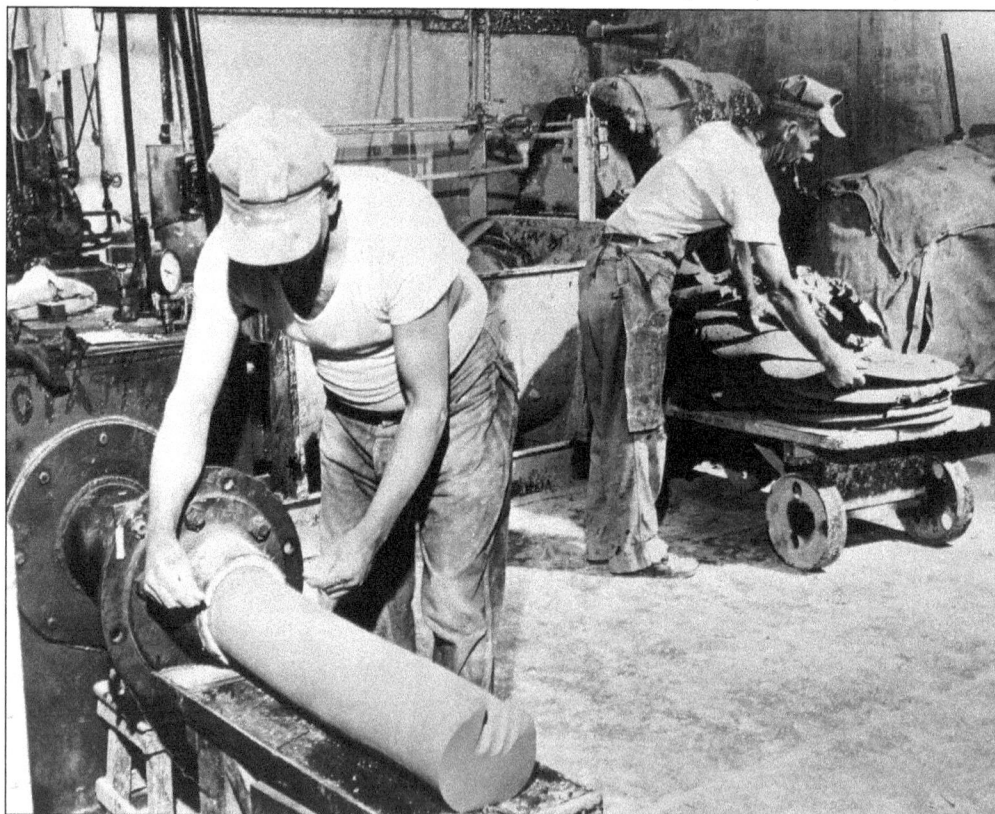

W.S. GEORGE STOCK, 1966. After bankruptcy reorganization in 1958, stocks were sold in an attempt to revive the company. Backers were found in Pennsylvania and local citizens and workers purchased stocks to give the company capital to continue. George T. McKinstry, president, and Ina Hartford, secretary, signed the stock form issued to Dorothy Jean Forney, the daughter of a retired bookkeeper and one of the photographers at the plant. Royal China of nearby Salem hired workers and continued to produce some W. S. George lines from 1959 through 1966. (Forney Collection.)

Certificate

FOR

20

SHARES

OF THE

COMMON STOCK

OF

The W. S. George Pottery Company

ISSUED TO

Dorothy Jean Forney

DATED

THE MORRIS BROTHERS STORE. Brothers William and Walter Morris opened a cash and carry grocery business in a room on Market Street in 1901. Three years later, they added a room and a line of dry goods. This photo shows the enlarged establishment after the brothers purchased the C. P. Rothwell Building in 1908. They added a second location north of the railroad depot in 1912. Walter supervised the new store, while William stayed at the Rothwell Building. The dry goods portion of the business was abandoned and the brothers devoted all their time to the grocery operation. (Morris Family Collection.)

MORRIS BROTHERS GROCERY, MARKET STREET. The Morris Brothers opened in a second location on South Market Street in 1923. It was later relocated to the First National Bank Building on North Market. A.L., another Morris brother, took over the South Market store in 1926 and operated it in conjunction with a grocery delivery service. William remained to assist with training. A.L. had previously opened two different meat markets in East Palestine beginning in 1912. Relatives of the Morris Family remain active in the grocery trade in the town today. (Morris Family Collection.)

EAST PALESTINE UNION SCHOOL. A special district was created in 1865, authorizing the selection of a board of education. This brick building was erected in 1875 at a cost of $14,000. 250 pupils from all grades attended schools under the direction of a principal and four teachers. (Gray Collection.)

W.S. GEORGE HOLIDAY PARTY, C. 1949. (Gray Collection.)

INDEPENDENT STITCHERY CLUB, C. 1949. Pictured from left to right are the following: (front row) Edna Helman, Ann Ward, Nell Handte, and Mary Todd; (back row) Lyde Nicely, Ethel Benton, Ella Ott, Mrs. Waymar, Maude Skinner, Mrs. Torhwell, Kathryn Conley, Mrs. Logan, Mrs. Farline, Luella Forney, Margaret Chapin, and Ina Hersh. (Forney Collection.)

McGraw Rubber Company. Important early industries in East Palestine were sawmills, carriage shops, grist mills, coal oil producers, and distilleries. Businesses were later established to manufacture rubber and steel products. Two major pottery companies were opened before the turn of the century. (Gray Collection.)

Modern-Day Post Office. The first post office in the town was established around 1836 in William Paxson's store, where Robert Chamberlain served as postmaster. During these early days, mail was brought on horseback from nearby Unity. (Gray Collection.)

Eight

CELEBRATING
THE FUTURE

FIESTAWARE. Floods, fire, changes in technology, and economic depressions all took heavy tolls on the pottery industry in the Ohio Valley, but the final challenges of foreign competition and the changing tastes in home fashion, including plastic and paper dinnerware, resulted in the precipitous decline in the number of works from the golden age near the turn of the century. Today nearly 2500 employees work at Sterling, Homer Laughlin, and Hall companies, as well as a number of smaller companies in the Ohio Valley. Some produce custom hand-decorated wares while others offer commercial and retail lines. Fiestaware, produced by Homer Laughlin, is contributing to a nationwide renaissance in dinnerware popularity. There are even a few potteries that continue to operate with one small lone kiln, exactly like the ones used in the beginnings of the industry. (Courtesy of the Homer Laughlin China Company.)

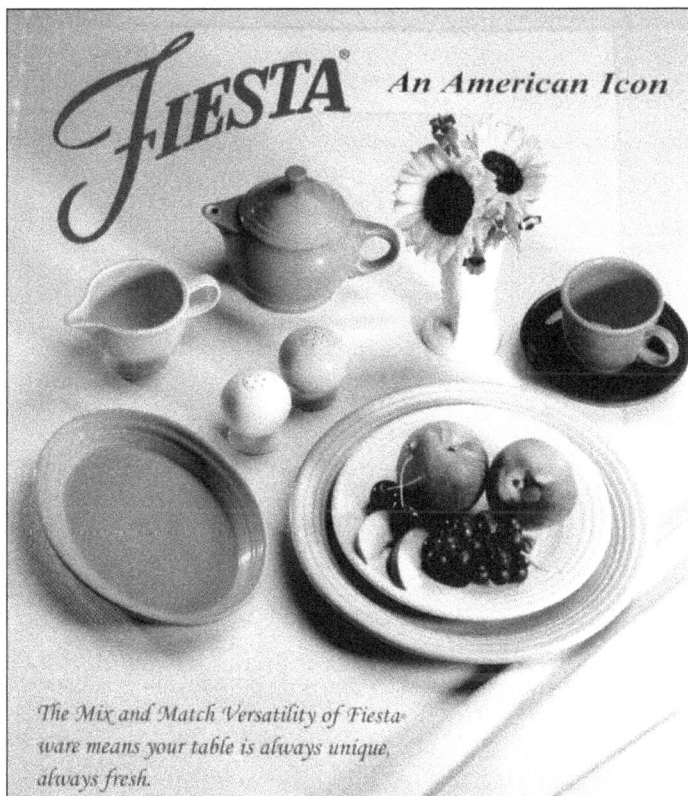

The Mix and Match Versatility of Fiesta ware means your table is always unique, always fresh.

FIESTA® SHAPES

~ All products are Lead Free ~

  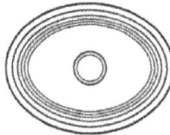 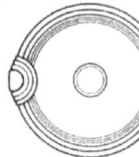 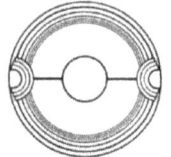

0463 Plate B & B 6-1/8"
0464 Plate Salad 7-1/4"
0465 Plate Luncheon 9"
0466 Plate Dinner 10-1/2"
0467 Plate Chop 11-3/4"
0505 Pizza Plate 15"

0760 Snack Plate w/well 10-1/2"

0456 Platter 9-5/8"
0457 Platter 11-5/8"
0458 Platter 13-5/8"
New 0409 Deep Oval Serving Platter 15-3/4"

0468 Round Serving Tray 11"

0753 Hostess Tray 12-1/4"

0765 Pedestal Bowl 9-7/8" 64 oz.

New
0460 Bowl Small 5-5/8" 14-1/4 oz.
0461 Bowl Medium 6-7/8" 19 oz.
0471 Bowl Large 8-1/4"
1 quart (40 oz.)
0455 Bowl Extra Large 2 quarts

0723 Gusto Bowl 23 oz.

0421 Small Mixing Bowl 7-1/2" 44 oz.
0422 Medium Mixing Bowl 8-1/2" 60 oz.
0482 Large Mixing Bowl 9-1/2" 70 oz.

0495 Covered Casserole 70 oz.

0451 Rim Soup 9" 13-1/4 oz.
0462 Pasta Bowl 12" 21 oz.

0459 Fruit 5-3/8" 6-1/4 oz.
0472 Stacking Cereal Bowl 6-1/2" 11 oz.

0450 Bouillon 6-3/4 oz.

0766 Tripod Bowl

0098 Chili Bowl 18 oz.

0750 Salt 2-1/4" x 2-5/8"
0751 Pepper 2-1/4" x 2-5/8"
0497 S & P Set

0756 Rangetop S & P

0470 Saucer 5-7/8"
0477 Saucer A.D. 4-7/8"
0293 Jumbo Saucer 6-3/4"

New

0549 Cup A.D. 3 oz.

0476 Cup A.D. 3 oz.

0452 Cup 7-3/4 oz.

0453 Mug 10-1/4 oz.

0149 Jumbo Cup 18 oz

0418 Cappucino Mug 21 oz

0424 Pedestal Mug 18 oz

0446 Tumbler 6-1/2 oz.

New

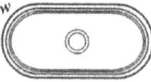

0412 Bread Tray 12" x 5-3/4"

0499 Relish/Utility Tray 9-1/2"

0473 Fiesta® Clock

0821 Sugar & Cream Tray Set

0498 Individual Cov. Sugar 8-3/4 oz.

0492 Individual Cream 7 oz.

New

0486 Sauceboat 18-1/2 oz.

0488 Round Candlestick Holder 3-5/8"

0430 Tapered Candlestick Holder 6"

0494 Covered Butter

0487 Deep Dish Pie Baker 10-1/4"
0417 Small Pie Baker 6-3/8"
0419 Medium Pie Baker 8-1/4"

0490 Bud Vase 6"

0491 Medium Vase 9-5/8"
New 0440 Small Vase 8"

0484 Disc Pitcher Lg. 67-1/4 oz.
0485 Disc Pitcher Sm. 28 oz.
0475 Miniature Disc Pitcher 5 oz.

0448 Carafe w/handle 60 oz.

0493 Covered Coffee 36 oz.

0496 Covered Teapot 44 oz.

0764 Teapot 2 Cup

New
0439 Spoon Rest 8"

THE HOMER LAUGHLIN CHINA CO.

Phone: 800/452-4462
Retail Outlet Fax: 304/ 387-4265

~ Made in the USA ~
Newell, WV 26050-1259

www.hlchina.com
hlc@hlchina.com

and "Fiesta" are registered trademarks of THE HOMER LAUGHLIN CHINA CO. Photographs, illustrations and specifications are based on current product information at time of publication. The right is reserved to make changes at any time without notice. Printed in U.S.A. 12/01

THE 2002 LINE OF HLLC FIESTAWARE. (Courtesy of the Homer Laughlin China Company.)

RESOURCES

Page constraints prohibit a complete scholarly bibliography. History of the pottery industry in the Ohio Valley can be found in various places. Area historical societies, libraries, and museums offer vast resources for the history of the cities and businesses. Collections at the Los Angeles and Allen County (Indiana) Libraries offer atlases, city directories, and county histories. This project would not have been possible without the resources of the Museum of Ceramics in East Liverpool. The displays, artifacts, and archives are invaluable in documenting the history of the city and of the pottery works. The museum should be the first stop for visitors to the area.

Homer Laughlin China Company in Newell, West Virginia and Hall China Company in East Liverpool, Ohio both offer guided tours of their plants. Sterling China Company of Wellsville and W.C. Bunting and Pioneer Pottery of East Liverpool continue to operate but are not open to the public. Brighton Falls China continues production of Mayer China in Beaver Falls, Pennsylvania, but does not offer tours. My sincere thanks to John Sayle of Hall China, Dave Conley of Homer Laughlin China, Bruce Hall of Sterling China, and Donald N. Hopper of Brighton Falls China for sharing information about their modern operations. Several small local companies continue to produce novelties and craftware and operate decorating firms in the tri-state area today.

The East Liverpool Chamber of Commerce offers maps and information about the area, pottery company tours, and the Tri-State Pottery Festival.

POTTERY.
CHARGING A KILN

EAST LIVERPOOL POST OFFICE, C. 1910. (Museum of Ceramics.)

THE MUSEUM OF CERAMICS, EAST LIVERPOOL, 2002. The heritage of the pottery industry in East Liverpool and the surrounding area is documented today at the Museum of Ceramics, located in the post office building at Fifth and Broadway, which is listed in the National Register of Historic Places. Supervised by the Ohio Historical Society, the museum houses the largest display of Lotus ware in the United States. (Gray Collection.)

FIESTA COMMEMORATIVE MINI PITCHER, 2002. Every June the Tri-State Pottery Festival is held to celebrate the past and the future of the pottery industry. Homer Laughlin China Company began creating souvenirs for the Tri-state Festival in 1993. Each piece is glazed with a new color and marked with the logo and date. Collector teapots were introduced in 2001. Each pot is a unique shape and is produced by a local pottery using a local designer. (Gray Collection.)

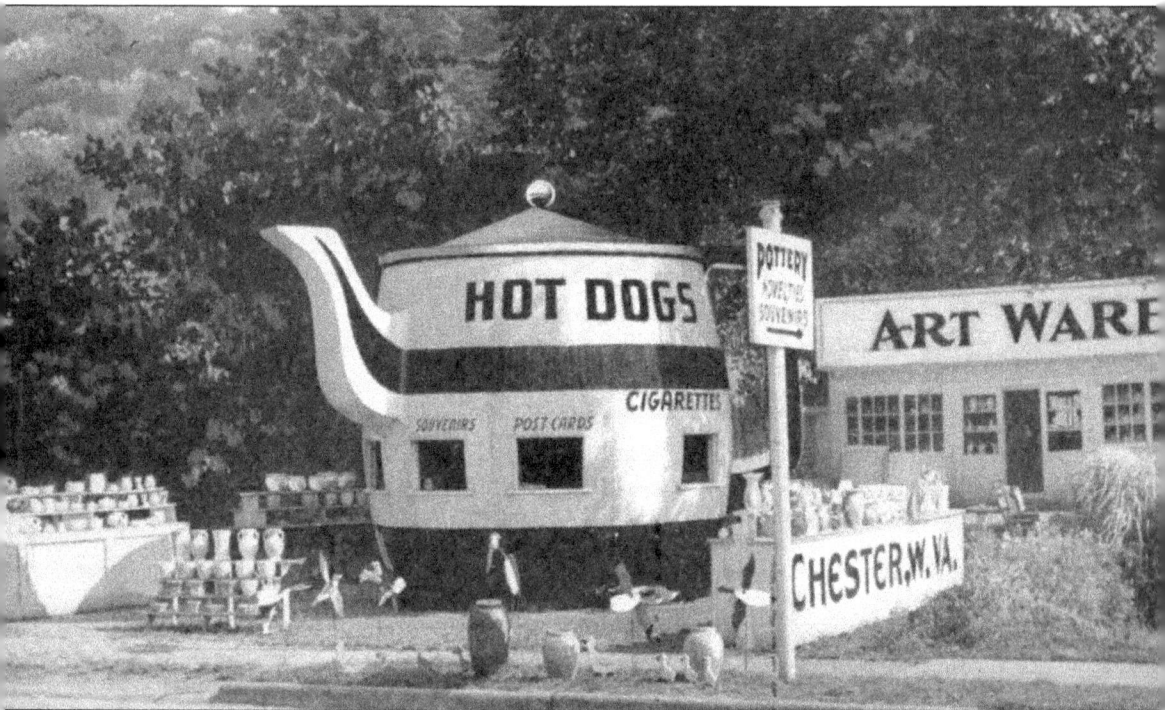

GIANT TEAPOT. On the top ten of the "World's Largest" lists, the Chester Teapot still can be seen in Chester. Originally designed as a wooden roadside novelty for Hires Rootbeer, the teapot was reinvented as a roadside pottery stand in the 1940s by William Devon. Today, the fenced teapot sits alone at the edge of the town after being relocated from its original site and restored by volunteers on a concrete pad donated by the Tri-State Pottery Festival Association. (Gray Collection.)

www.ingramcontent.com/pod-product-compliance
Lightning Source LLC
Chambersburg PA
CBHW050710110426
42813CB00007B/2140